Pasquale J. Simonelli, Ph.D.

ENRICO CARUSO
Unedited Notes

The 1901-17 never published before and here reproduced correspondence between the Italian tenor Enrico Caruso and an Italian family in New York City.

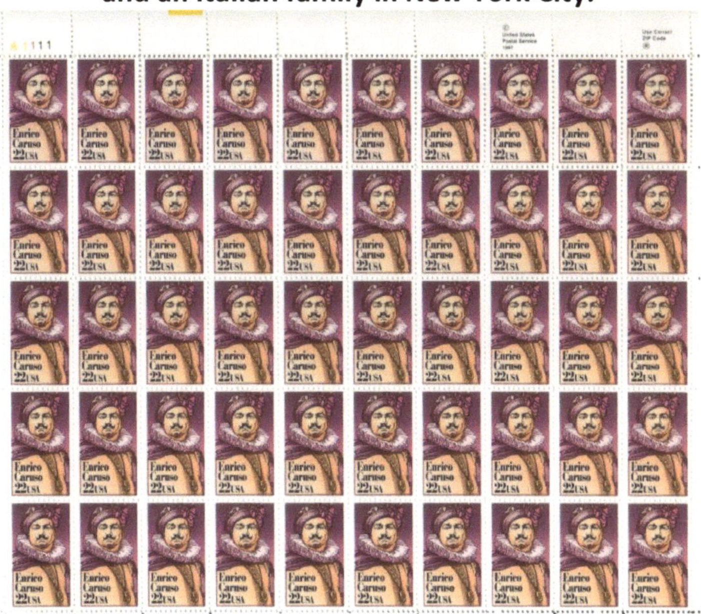

Sacer Equestris Aureus Ordo

ISBN-13: 978-0615714905

ISBN-10: 0615714900

Sacer Equestris Aureus Ordo Inc.
Music division
Charleston, SC, USA

To my Grandfather
Comm. Pasquale I. Simonelli,
who introduced me to the *bel canto.*

CONTENT

PREFACE

The beautiful singing, *il bel canto*, became the memory of the past glory of Italy since the first performance of Verdi's opera *Nabucco*, in 1842 at *La Scala* in Milan. The instant success of its *"Chorus of the Hebrew Slaves,"*[1]

"Va, pensiero,	"Fly, thought,
sull'ali dorate..."	on golden wings..."

Italian opera singing awoke in the patriotic souls the greatness of their

"Patria	"Mother Country
sì bella e perduta!	so beautiful and lost!
Oh membranza	Oh, remembrance
sì cara e fatal!"	so dear and so dire!"

Opera arias became messengers of Italian culture throughout the World.

A 1919 very popular Neapolitan song, *Santa Lucia Luntana,*[2] (Distant Santa Lucia), a romantic and panoramic locality in Naples, Italy, describes the sadness of emigrants:

"Partono e bastimenti	"On boats leaving
per terre assai luntane,	for very remote lands,
cantano a buordo	there is singing on board,
so' napulitane."	they are Neapolitans."

Who, among the Italians living abroad at that time, was not moved and proud at the same time, while

[1] Third act.
[2] E. A. Mario.

listening and singing the words and the melodies of their heritage? The longing they felt for their native land, was beautifully expressed by the famous Neapolitan song *Torn'à Surriento* (Come back to Sorrento). It was composed in New York City by Ernesto De Curtis in 1902. It remembers his honeymoon with his wife Amalia spent in that locality on the Gulf of Naples. The song glorifies Sorrento, as the land of love (*terra de l'ammore*). Therefore, how could you have the heart of not coming back (*tiene 'o core 'e nun turnà*)? Do not leave me (*nun me lassà*), come back to Sorrento (*torn'à Surriento*), make me live (*famme campà*)!

At a time when Italians in America were despised as pariahs, befriending opera singers and promoting them in America was a way of keeping alive and contributing to the advancement of Italian awareness in the United States.

An inedited series of original postcards,[3] exchanged between a New York Italian family and the great tenor Enrico Caruso,[4] offer an example of these events and feelings.

Mr. Francis Robinson, Assistant Manager of the Metropolitan Opera of New York City, in a 1964 letter to the author of this book, refers that "Caruso seems to have been very fond of postcards and even addressed them to

---

[3] A July 1964 gift of Mr. Francis Robinson (Assistant Manager of the Metropolitan Opera, NY in 1970) to the author's family. *Cf.* Robinson, *CARUSO, HIS LIFE IN PICTURES*.

[4] Born in Naples, Italy on February 25, 1873, died in Naples on August 2, 1921.

himself." Along with that same letter, he gave us the gift of the postcards published in this book. He wrote, "Here are some cards from your family to the great man [*i.e.* Caruso] I have long wanted to send you. You will notice they wrote in series, numbering them." No mention is made on how Mr. Robinson got them.

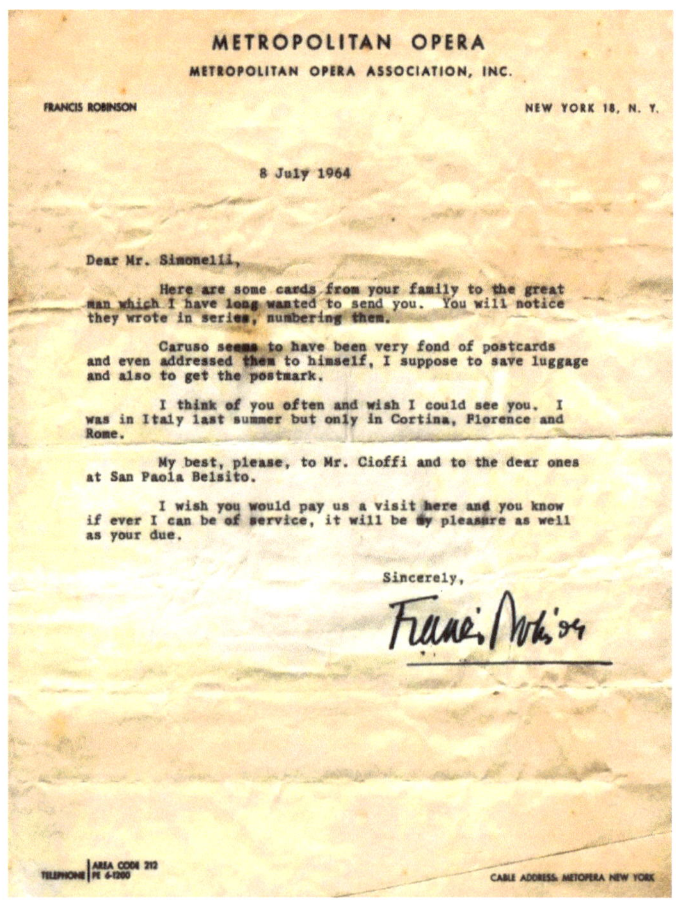

METROPOLITAN OPERA
METROPOLITAN OPERA ASSOCIATION, INC.

FRANCIS ROBINSON — NEW YORK 18, N. Y.

8 July 1964

Dear Mr. Simonelli,

Here are some cards from your family to the great man which I have long wanted to send you. You will notice they wrote in series, numbering them.

Caruso seems to have been very fond of postcards and even addressed them to himself, I suppose to save luggage and also to get the postmark.

I think of you often and wish I could see you. I was in Italy last summer but only in Cortina, Florence and Rome.

My best, please, to Mr. Cioffi and to the dear ones at San Paola Belsito.

I wish you would pay us a visit here and you know if ever I can be of service, it will be my pleasure as well as your due.

Sincerely,

Francis Robinson

TELEPHONE | AREA CODE 212 PE 6-1200 — CABLE ADDRESS: METOPERA NEW YORK

Besides those postcards, the telegrams, letters and documents, reproduced in this book, were retrieved among the papers of Pasquale I. Simonelli. He had saved them as a memento of the friendship between him and Enrico Caruso.

The correspondence with the tenor started on February 22, 1901 with a postcard of the Brooklyn Bridge, New York. In it, the writer states that he had "the sweet memory of his very beautiful voice" (*il dolce ricordo della sua bellissima voce*) heard in Naples, Italy. Furthermore, he declares of being aware that Caruso "desired to collect commemorative postcards" (*desiderava fare una collezione di cartoline commemorative*). Therefore, he took upon himself to start this communication.

Eventually, the correspondence with the tenor transformed in friendship. Ultimately it became instrumental for Caruso's engagement at the New York Metropolitan Opera in 1903.

***

Commemorative stamps:

La Scala Italy 1978 Metropolitan Opera US 1983

Italy 1973

US 1987

Enrico Caruso, in both stamps, as
the Duke of Mantua, in Verdi's *Rigoletto*.

***

On June 1903, from Buenos Aires,
Caruso writes to Pasquale I. Simonelli,

oggi scrivo alla mia signora che vi mandi una fotografia

"... Today I write to my wife that
she may send you a photograph..."

Enrico Caruso (1903),
"With felt thanks and greetings Caruso"

Caruso's brief biographical notes

Early life

Enrico Caruso was born on February 25, 1873 in Naples, Italy. He was the third child of seven siblings. At age 11 he followed the trade of his father, Marcellino, as a casting worker. His mother, Anna Baldini Caruso, encouraged his normal education and his singing lessons at age 16. He sung in churches' choirs, as entertainer in cafés, in restaurants and in the streets.

Singing career

After a shaky beginning at a Neapolitan theater, the tenor Caruso landed a contract with *La Scala* in Milan and other Italian cities.

From 1895 to 1920, Caruso was engaged in London (*Covent Garden*), in Saint Petersburg (*Mariinsky* Theatre), in Moscow (*Bolshoi* Theatre), in Buenos Aires (Teatro *Colón*). in New York (*Metropolitan Opera House*), in San Francisco (*Grand Opera House*) and many other cities throughout the United States and the world.

He sang in Argentina, Austria, Brazil, Belgium, Canada, Cuba, France, Germany, Hungary, Mexico, Monaco, Portugal and Uruguay. At the Metropolitan Opera House in New York, he sang for 18 seasons and had 863 appearances'

Family life

For 11 years (1897-1906), Caruso lived with Ada Giachetti, an Italian soprano who had left her previous marriage to follow the great tenor. They had four sons, but only two survived, Rodolfo and Enrico.

In 1918 Caruso married Dorothy Park Benjamin, a 25 year old aristocratic New Yorker, and they had a daughter, Gloria.

In 1904, Caruso purchased his Italian new home, the majestic and sumptuous Villa Bellosguardo near Florence. While in New York City, he resided, among other hotels, at the Knickerbocker Hotel suite. Near Naples, he lived in his suite at the Hotel Excelsior in Sorrento.

Business wisdom

It was not only Caruso's great voice and talent that gave him the international success he deserved. It was also his business acumen and his understanding of the great potentiality offered by the new technologies available.

Caruso understood the great opportunity presented by the sound recording. In fact, he was the first singer in history to sell, in 1904, one million copies of his *Vesti la giubba*, an aria from Leoncavallo's *Pagliacci*.

From that date to 1920 Caruso amassed a fortune in millions of dollars from his 260 and more recordings with the "*Gramophone & Typewriter Company*" and then with the "*Victor Talking Machine Company*" (RCA).

He also radio-broadcasted live from the Metropolitan Opera House. In addition, he appeared in two silent films. During World War I, Caruso gave concerts to raise money for the troops and the cause of war.

Impeccably elegant, Caruso had become the idol of more than half a million Italian immigrants living in New York City at the time. The Italian king, Victor Emmanuel III, bestowed upon him the dignity of *Cavaliere della Corona d'Italia*, Chevalier of the Italian Crown.

Illnesses and last days

Heavy smoking, sedentary life, overload of work, all contributed to Caruso's health deterioration, which started while he was still at the Metropolitan Opera House. Many episodes of illness, bronchitis, migraines and hemorrhages manifested themselves also on stage, during his performances.

Caruso went back to Italy and there, in Naples, at the Hotel Vesuvio, he died with a lung infection on August 2, 1921, he was 48 years old.

CHAPTER 1
Postcards from Giovanni in Caruso's personal collection

Giovanni Simonelli,[5] the writer of some of the postcards collected by Caruso, left Naples, Italy at the age of 26. He traveled on the ship Alesia[6] and arrived in New York on May 27, 1892. Eventually, he settled in New York City. There he founded a money exchange and travel agency company, together with his half-brother James, the *G. Simonelli & Bros*, at 70 Spring Street, New York.[7]

In 1890, Giovanni Simonelli had met tenor Vincenzo De Salvin[8] at the Sannazaro Theatre of Naples. De Salvin wrote to Giovanni from the Teatro Nazionale di Catania, where he was engaged in 1897 for Verdi's *La forza del destino*. The tenor informed him that Enrico Caruso desired to collect commemorative post cards.

Giovanni had heard Caruso in 1894 at the theater Mercadante in Naples, Italy. He wrote to the tenor, in Via Velasco, N.1, Milan, Italy, his first sequence of cards.[9] He numbered each one, serialized them and mailed each series in bulk.

---

[5] Born on April 11, 1865 in Saviano (Naples) - died on March 30, 1941 at San Paolo Belsito (Naples). *Cf. familylink* # 0451 record ID 367657.

[6] ID 82116.

[7] *Cf.* De Biasi, *Il Carroccio...*, ad. V.7, n.1, p. 13.

[8] *Cf.* De Felice, *VITTORIA COLONNA...*, p. 655.

[9] *Cf.* Key, *Enrico Caruso a biography*, pp. 168, 170.

Giovanni Simonelli, June 3 1908 in NYC.

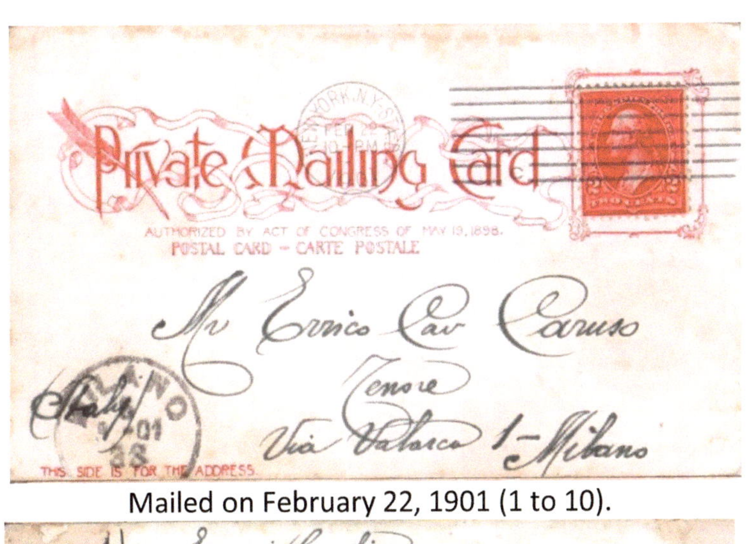

Mailed on February 22, 1901 (1 to 10).

1) Egregio Cavaliere,
Il Tenore Sig.r De Salvin mi scrisse che lei desidera fare una collezione di cartoline commemorative, ed io con piacere adempio.

BROOKLYN BRIDGE, NEW YORK.
COPYRIGHT 1895 BY A. LOEFFLER N.Y.
Arthur Strauss, Inc., Publishers, New York No. 103
Indirizzo 29 E. 3d Street
New York 22 Febbraio 901 -

Brooklyn Bridge, New York

"1) New York February 22, 1901 address 29 East 3rd Street

Distinguished Chevalier, tenor Mr. De Salvin, wrote to me that you wish to collect commemorative postcards, and I comply willingly..."

PRIVATE MAILING CARD.
Authorized by Act of Congress of May 19th, 1898.
(POSTAL CARD—CARTE POSTALE.)

Mr Enrico Cav Caruso
Tenore
Via Velasca 1
Milano
(Italy)

THIS SIDE IS EXCLUSIVELY FOR THE ADDRESS

MADISON SQUARE AND FIFTH AVENUE, NEW YORK.

2) al di lei desiderio, siccome è in me sempre vivo il dolce ricordo della sua bellissima voce che tanto mi entusiasmo parecchi anni or sono al Fondo di Napoli - D'allora io non ho avuto più la fortuna di sentirlo, però dai

"2) ...to your wish since it is always vivid in me the sweet memory of your very beautiful voice that enthused me very much many years ago at the Fondo of Naples[10] - Since then I did not have the fortune to hear you again, however from.."

---

[10] Teatro Mercadante, during the 1894 performance of Thomas' *Mignon*. After that performance, Caruso was fired. Nevertheless, Giovanni realized that the tenor had a great voice.

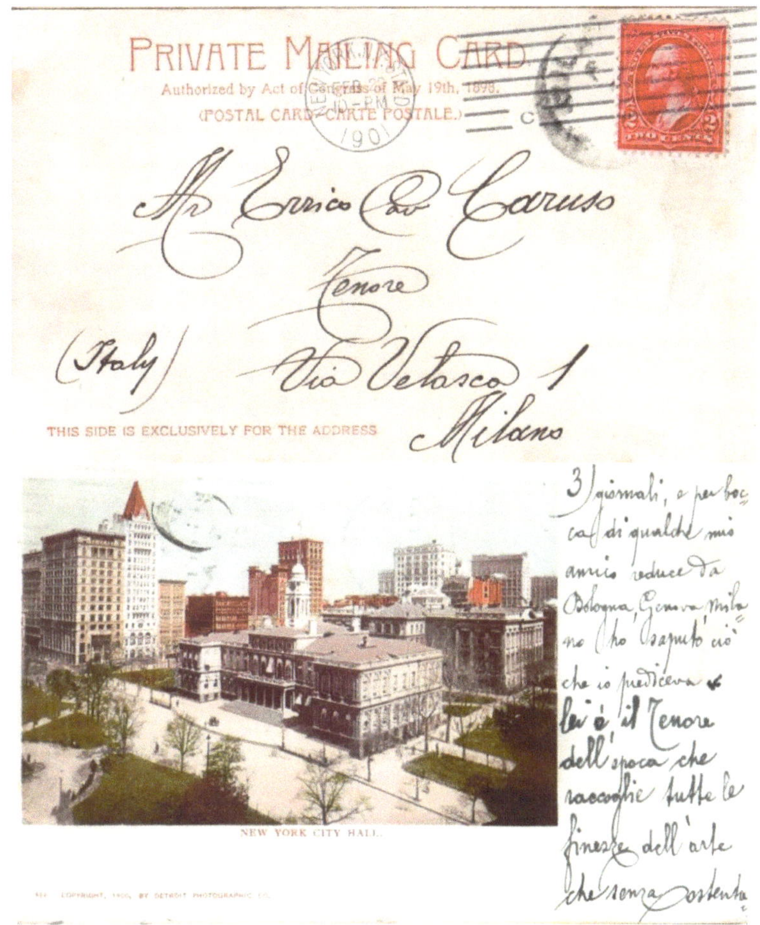

PRIVATE MAILING CARD
Authorized by Act of Congress of May 19th, 1898.
(POSTAL CARD—CARTE POSTALE.)

Mr Enrico Cav Caruso
Tenore
(Italy) Via Velasca 1
Milano

THIS SIDE IS EXCLUSIVELY FOR THE ADDRESS

NEW YORK CITY HALL

3) giornali, e per boc
ca di qualche mio
amico reduce da
Bologna, Genova, Mila
no (ho saputo ciò
che io prediceva e
lei è il Tenore
dell'epoca che
raccoglie tutte le
finezze dell'arte
che senza ostenta

"3) ...the newspapers, and by word of mouth of some friend coming from Bologna, Genoa, Milan (I came to know what I predicted that you are the Tenor of the century that possesses all the refinements of the art that without ostenta[tion]...*"*

H) rione puó chiamarsi celeb
SYNDICATE BUILDING
VIEW OF BROADWAY TAKEN FROM
CITY HALL PARK SHOWING
SYNDICATE BUILDING 32 STORIES HIGH
Arthur Strauss, Publisher, New York. No. 8.

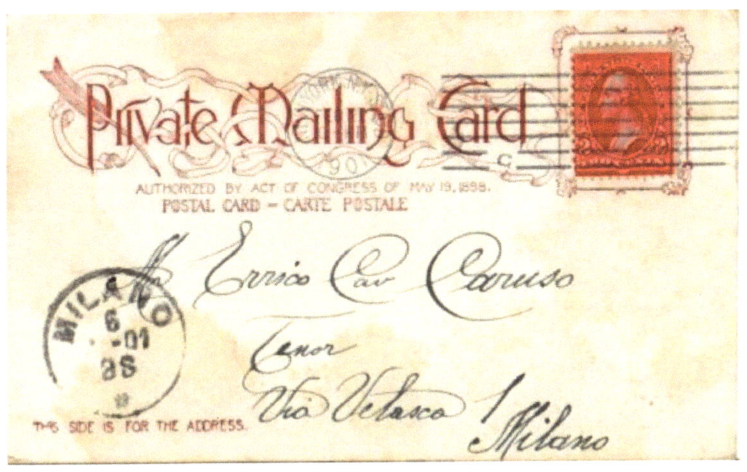

"*4)*... [ostenta]*tion can be called celebrity*... "

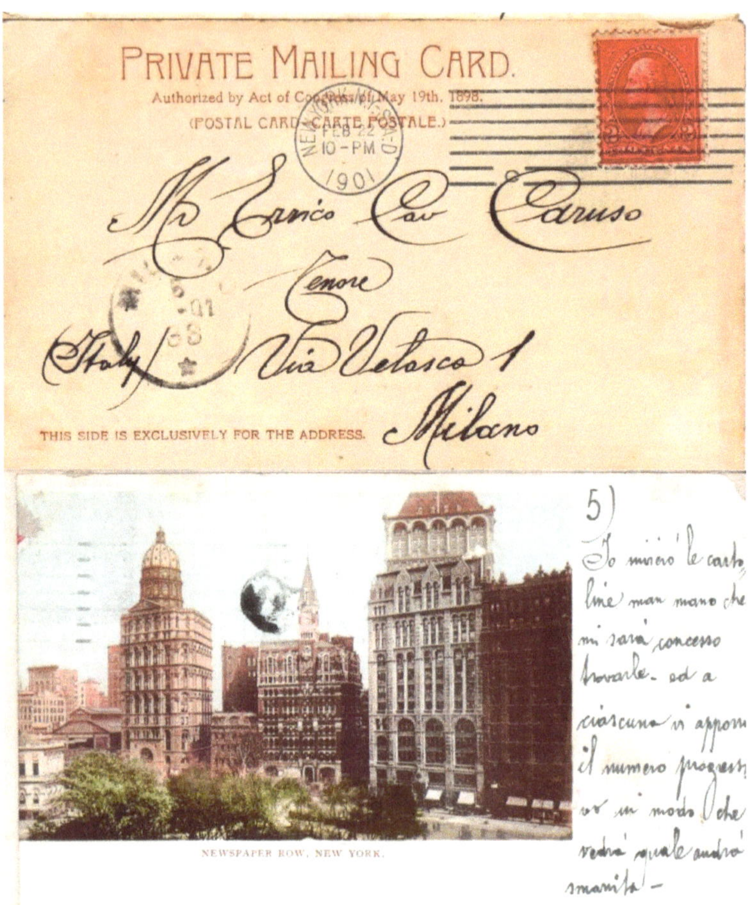

NEWSPAPER ROW, NEW YORK.

"5) ...I will send the postcards as I will be able to find them - and to each I will put a progressive number so that you will see which one went lost - ..."

"6) ...I make it a point if I can be of help in anything, and with sincere wishes I give you my best regards begging you to extend them also to Mr. De Salvin.

Yours very devout Giovanni Simonelli 29 E. 3rd Street New York."

Monday, February 4, 1901, the Metropolitan Opera House of New York City presented for the first time Puccini's opera *Tosca* under the direction of the international Italian conductor Luigi Mancinelli.[11] The Croatian soprano Katarina Milka T(e)rnina sang the role of Tosca.

Milka Ternina as the title role in Puccini's *Tosca*.
Photo: Aimé Dupont [12]

The Italian baritone Antonio Scotti[13] sang the role of Scarpia and the Italian tenor Giuseppe Cremonini[14] sang the role of Mario.

---

[11] 1848-1921.

[12] T(e)rnina (1863-1941) in that role. *Wikipedia* public domain photo.

[13] 1866-1936.

[14] 1866-1903.

"7) Monday was the premier of Tosca. It was a true success for maestro Puccini - Very dramatic..."

"8) ...was Ternina - Excellent Scotti - Good Cremonini..."

"9)...Excellent the orchestra directed by Mancinelli. Tonight I will go back to hear it and..."

"10) ...in this moment maestro Avitabile[15] *is playing for me a few notes: Recondite armonie di bellezze insiem*[16]*.... Yours truly G. Simonelli 29. E. 3rd St. New York."*

---

[15] Maestro of the New York's Metropolitan Opera House.

[16] *Sic. "Recondita armonia di bellezze diverse!"* (Concealed harmony of different beauties)" 1st verse of the homonymous aria sang by Mario, while painting a portrait of a lady and comparing it to the beauty of Tosca (Act I – scene 3). *Sic. Bellezze insiem* (beauties together) is in the 5th verse].

Mailed on February 26, 1901 (11 to 14).

"11) Distinguished Chevalier, I mailed you 10 of these - keep an eye on the progressive number - Which operas are you currently singing? What do you think of "Le Maschere"[17] - from the news..."

---

[17] In 1900, this opera buffa, with a Prologue and three acts by Pietro Mascagni, was not very well received in the Italian opera houses (in Genoa the performance was suspended).

Private Mailing Card.
(Authorized by Act of Congress of May 19, 1898.)
("POSTAL CARD, CARTE POSTALE.")
Henry Chev. Caruso Esq
Tenor
Via Velasca -1-
Milan
Italy.
THIS SIDE IS EXCLUSIVELY FOR THE ADDRESS.
12) nali che arrivano di costì: nulla si può dedurre - sono in completo disaccordo. Chi la ha cantata in Milano?
CENTRE STREET, NEW YORK

"12) ...papers that arrive here, nothing can be deducted - they are completely in disaccord - Who sang it in Milano?..."

"13) Tosca also for the second time was very well liked. Scotti and Termina were excellent - they raised enthusiasm - Cremonini, as usual gracious..."

(14

È vero che l'anno venturo sarà scritturato da Gesù per cantare qui? Se è così le manderò alcune norme in modo che abbia conoscenza di tutto prima di firmare il contratto.

MADISON SQUARE GARDEN
152 (NEW YORK)

Qui si eseguiscono corse di cavalli ciclistiche, pugilato, ecc ecc insomma tutto ciò che è sport. G. Simonelli

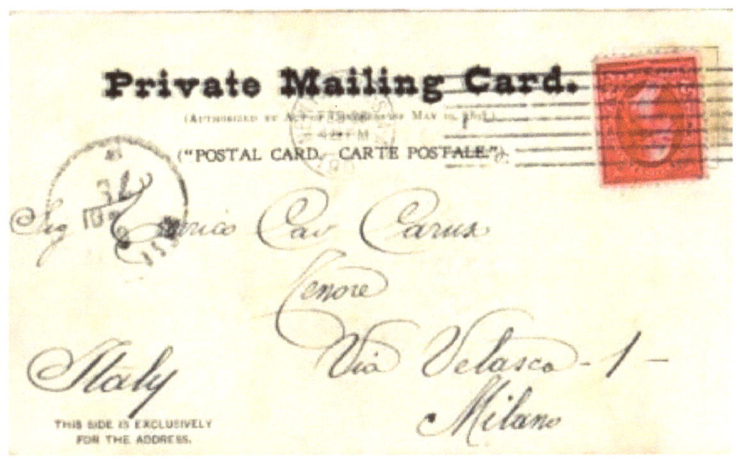

"14) ...Is it true that next year you will be engaged by Grau[18] *to sing here? If so I will send you some norms so that you will be able to know everything before signing the contract."*

[Referring to the Madison Square Garden depicted in the postcard; Giovanni writes,]

"Here are performed horse [and] *bicycle races, boxing, etc., etc. in short all that is sport.*
G. Simonelli"

 **Post cards numbers 15, 16 and 17 are missing.**

---

[18] Maurice Grau (1892–1903) was the general manager of the Metropolitan Opera House of New York City.

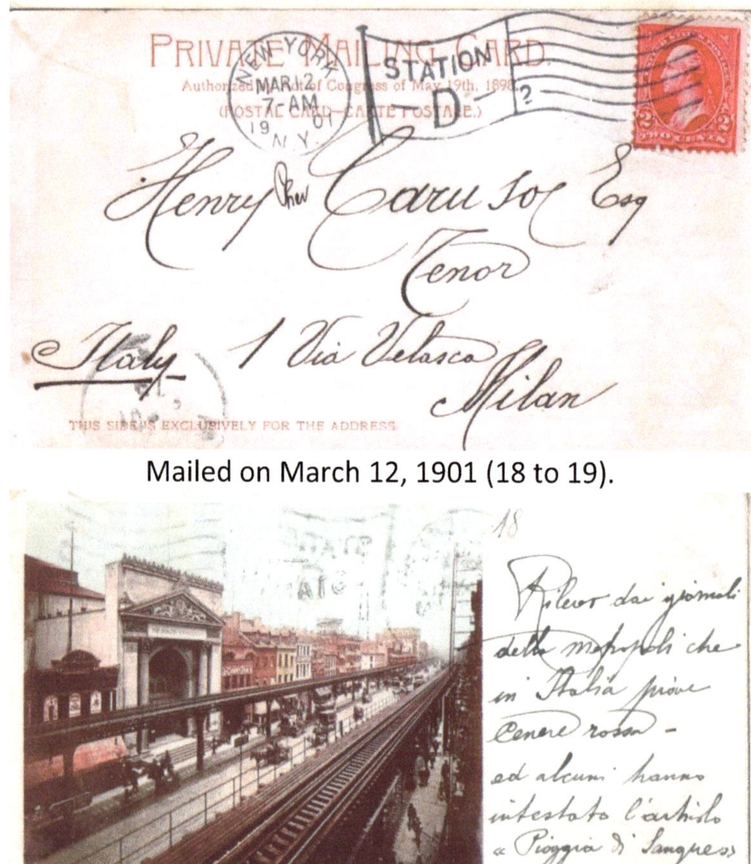

Mailed on March 12, 1901 (18 to 19).

"18) I learn from the metropolitan newspapers that in Italy[19] rain red ashes - and someone headed the article 'Rain of Blood.'..."

---

[19] March 12th, 1901 at Avellino, Naples, Italy.

"19) ...Best wishes and regards Very devoutly G. Simonelli"

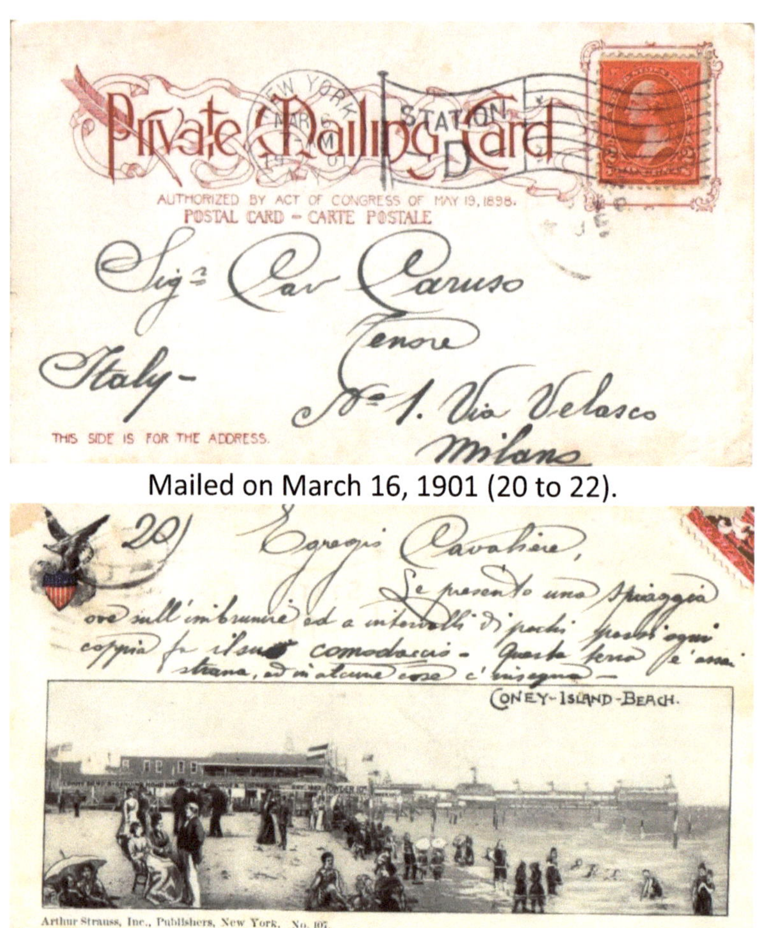

Mailed on March 16, 1901 (20 to 22).

"20) Distinguished Chevalier, I am presenting to you a beach where at dusk and with intervals of few steps every couple does whatever the heck pleases them. This land is very strange, and in something teaches us...."

PARK ROW BUILDING, NEW YORK.

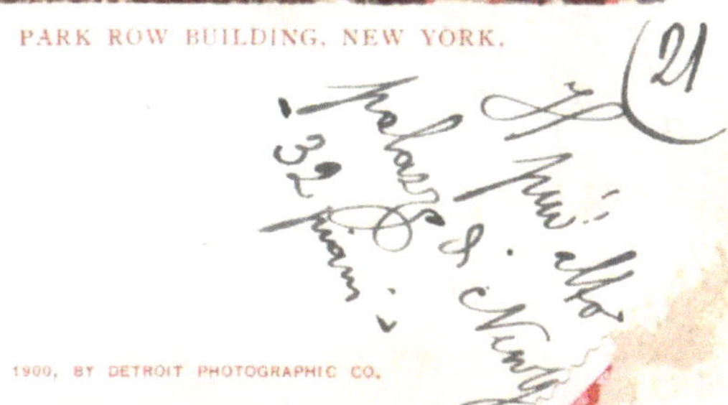

468 COPYRIGHT, 1900, BY DETROIT PHOTOGRAPHIC CO.

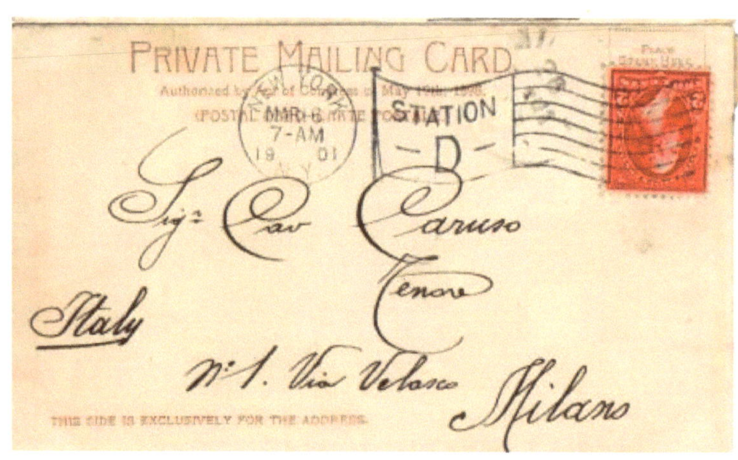

"21) The tallest building of New York - 32 floors."

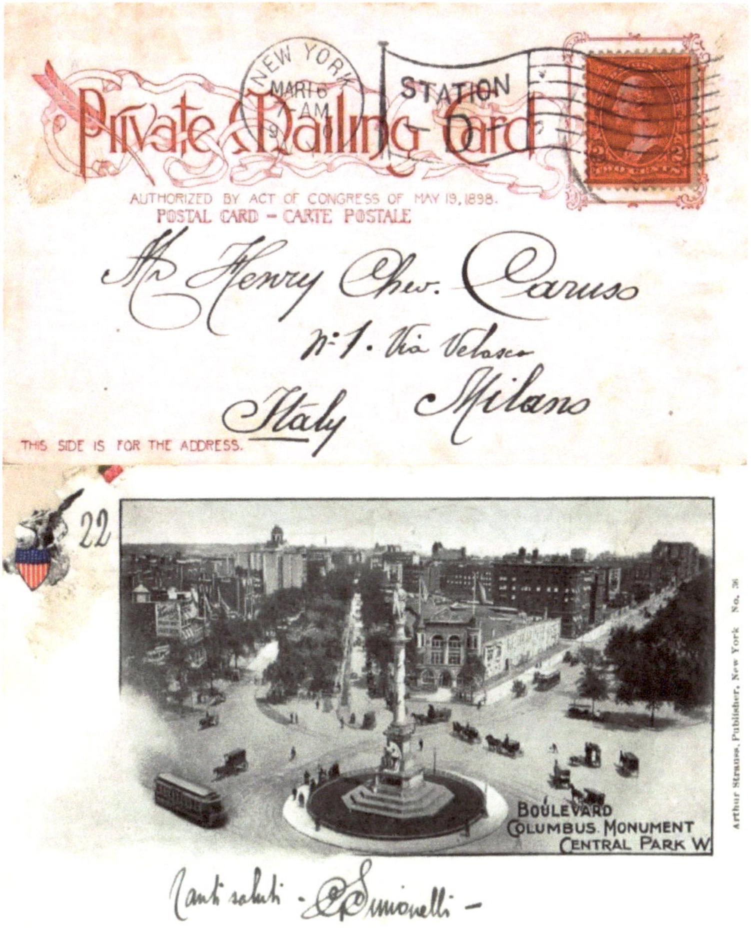

"22) Best regards G Simonelli"

 **Post card number 23 is missing.**

Mailed on March 19, 1901 (24 to 26).

"24) "Bohème" obtained a great success.[20] *Relatively to the Terrace* [in the postcard], *at the place I am writing there is a small lake* -..."

---

[20] March 1901 performance of Puccini's *"La Bohème."*

"25) ...Best regards - G Simonelli"

"26) Melba[21] *was an unsurpassed Mimi = Cremonini as voice is better placed than Saleza-*[22] *excellent always Campanari-*[23] *Scotti in the role of Tonio in Pagliacci*[24] *was very great the same in Don Giovanni-"*[25]

---

[21] Nellie Helen Porter Mitchell(1856-1931), Australian soprano.
[22] Luc Albert Saleza (1867-1916), Belgian tenor.
[23] Giuseppe Campanari (1855 – 1927), Italian baritone.
[24] By Leoncavallo.
[25] By Mozart.

Post card number 27 is missing.

Mailed on April 4, 1901 (28 to 32).

"28) NY April 3 1901. Distinguished Mr. Caruso, With great pleasure I received your two postcards and especially it was dear to me to receive also the two beautiful photographs. In the one without mustaches you are greatly transformed and having shown it to a lady..."

We do not know what were the lady's remarks since

postcard number 29 is missing

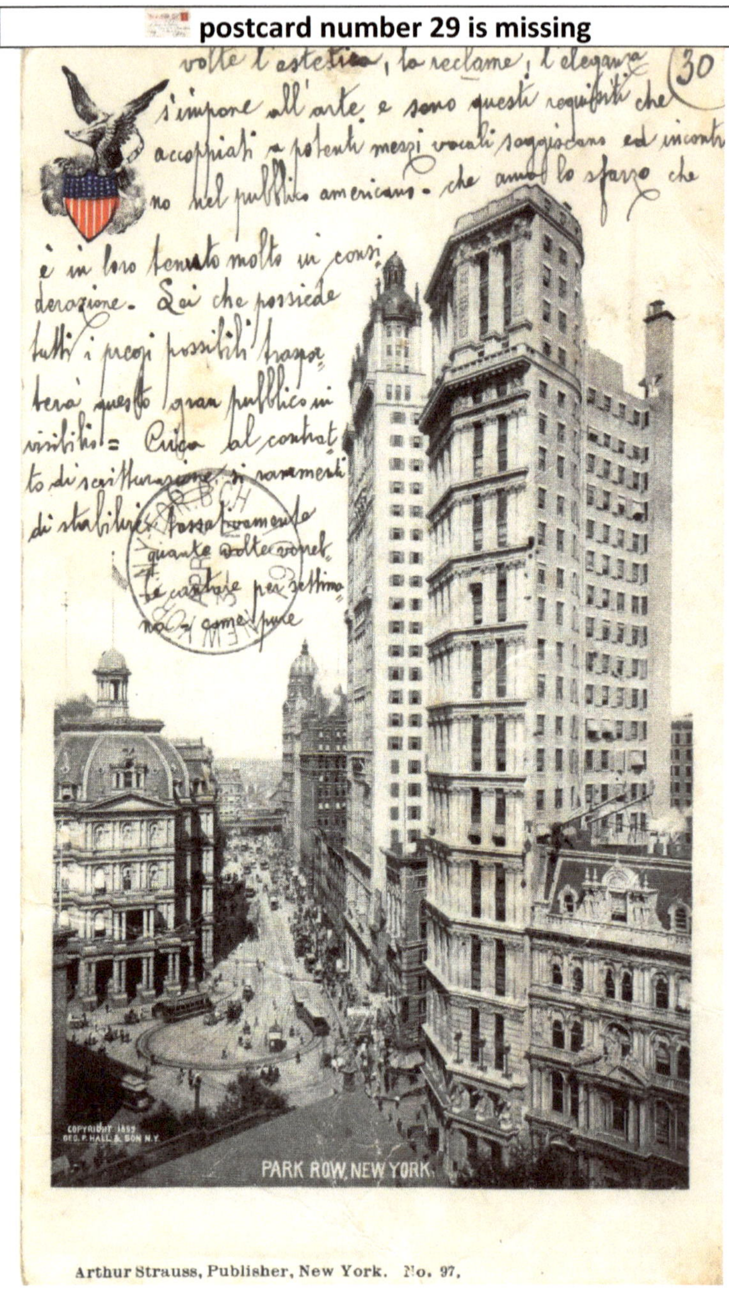

30

volte l'estetica, la reclame, l'eleganza
s'impone all'arte e sono questi requisiti che
accoppiati a potenti mezzi vocali soggiogano ed incontra-
no nel pubblico americano - che ama lo sfarzo che
è in loro tenuto molto in consi-
derazione. Lei che possiede
tutti i pregi possibili traspor-
terà questo gran pubblico in
visibilio = Circa al contratto di scritturazione, si rammenti
di stabilire tassativamente
quante volte vorrei
sentirla cantare per settimana, come pure

Arthur Strauss, Publisher, New York. No. 97.

"30) ...at times, aesthetics, publicity, elegance imposes itself on art and these are the requisites that pared with powerful vocal means subjugate and meet with the American public - that loves ostentation which is kept by them in great consideration. You that possess all the possible good qualities will throw into rapture this great public.

Regarding the engagement contract remember to establish precisely how many times a week you would want to sing and also..."

Private Mailing Card

AUTHORIZED BY ACT OF CONGRESS OF MAY 19, 1898.
POSTAL CARD — CARTE POSTALE

Sig.r Enrico Cav. Caruso
Tenore
Via Velasca N° 1
Milano
Italy

THIS SIDE IS FOR THE ADDRESS.

WORLD SUN & TRIBUNE BUILDINGS, N.Y.

Arthur Strauss, Publisher, New York No. 20.

si ricordi, e questo appunto è ciò che io l'avrei
mai in altra mia, cioè di fare un contratto in
scudi e non in lire siccome lo scudo che è
£5 italiane si spende in america ne più ne meno di
come la lira in Italia, cosicchè procuri di ottenere
ciò che esibisce in lire in Italia uguale somma
in dollari per l'america —
Sabato fu l'ultima della
Compagnia d'Opera - Nel Rigoletto la Melba
Cremonini e Campanari furono entusiasti = seguì
la Cavalleria e Scotti nella sua breve parte di
alfio fu ottimo e caratteristico nell'andatura da ca
rettiere = non avendogli dato il tempo giusto una
bestia di maestro tedesco di nome Flon nel duetto con Alfio così non
perdono ec. - invece di rivolgersi a Santuzza coi pugni stett

"31) ...remember, and this is indeed what I was referring to in another letter of mine, namely to write a contract in scudi not in lire since the scudo which is Italian ₤5[26] can be spent in America no more nor less that the lira in Italy, therefore make sure to obtain what you oblige in Italy in lire an equal amount in dollars for America -

Saturday was the last day for the *Compagnia d'Opera*.[27] In *Rigoletto*[28] Melba, Cremonini and Campanari were enthusiastic = followed *La cavalleria*[29] and Scotti in the brief role of Alfio was excellent and characteristic in the manner of a cart driver - not having given him the right tempo a beast of German director named Flon,[30] in the duet "*Ad essi non perdono*..."[31] instead of turning to Santuzza with tight fists..."

[26] Scudo, Franc *ecu*, Italian monetary denomination until 1900: = $1 US gold dollar = ₤5.18 Italian Liras = ₣5.18 French Francs.

[27] *Compagnia d'Opera* italiana.

[28] By Verdi.

[29] Mascagni's *La cavalleria rusticana*.

[30] M. Flon, *cf.* Krehbiel, *Chapters of opera*..., pp. 307, 309, 415.

[31] "I do not forgive them..." Act 1, scene 4.

si rivolse al Direttore a marcare così il suo sbaglio – Per quanto cercano di far trionfare la musica Tedesca, quest'anno la Boheme e la Tosca si sono imposte e schiettamente esse hanno fatto assai furore e tutti anelano risentirle – I veri Americani non vogliono musica Tedesca, ma questa città è cosmopolita e la colonia Tedesca s'impone ed è perciò che si hanno molte opere in questa lingua, ma all'americano d'America non va a sangue –

Ieri sera incontrai ad una festa il Tenore Beduschi che udii nel '94 a Verona nella Manon Lescaut e mi piacque assai – ora è qui senza veruna buona aspettativa – – Ho dato commissione per avere le cartoline da lei indicatemi e m'auguro che questo suo desiderio verrà appagato – Mando queste ed altre ancora del genere siccome acquistate tutte in una volta – Mi è capitato un giornale italiano [fra] le mani ed ivi letto che canta il Mefistofele con gran successo – bravo Ham

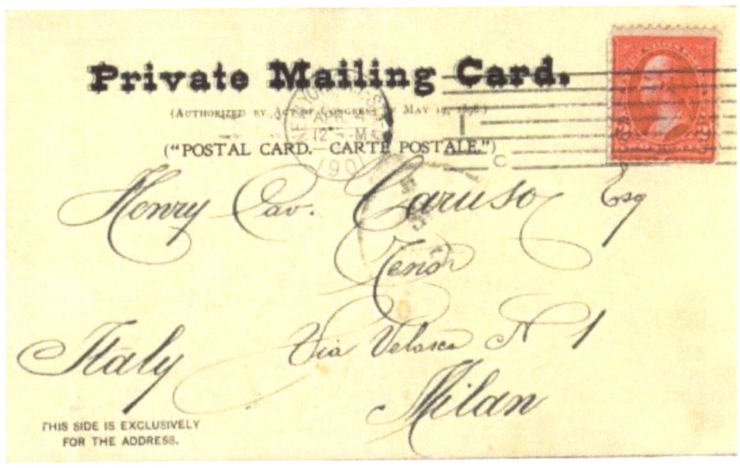

"32) ... he turned to the Director in order to highlight his mistake. As much as they try to promote German music, this year Bohème and Tosca imposed themselves and they were clearly a great success and everyone desires to hear them again. True Americans do not want German music, but this city is cosmopolitan and the German colony imposes itself and therefore we have many operas in this language, but it is not congenial to the American of America.

Last night at a party I met tenor Beduschi[32] *whom I heard in 1894 in Verona in Manon Lescaut*[33] *and I liked him very much. Now he is here without any expectation. -*

---

[32] Italian tenor Umberto Beduschi (1855-1920) was one of the first tenors for the role of De Grieux in Puccini's *Manon*. He became a voice professor at the *Chicago Conservatory of Music*.

[33] By Giacomo Puccini.

I commissioned the postcards you indicated and I hope this wish of yours will be fulfilled. I am sending this one and also more of this type since I bought them all at once. - I came across an Italian newspaper and I realized that you are singing Mefistofele [34] with great success.- Bravo. Bravo."

The next two postcards were mailed on May 31, 1901, without number.

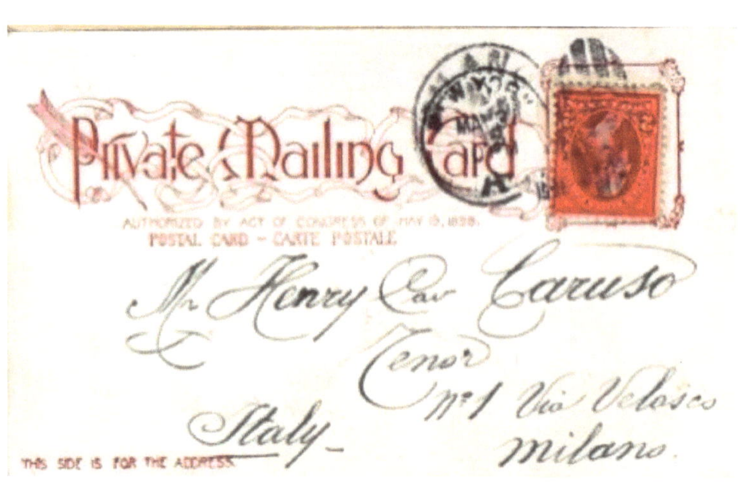

[34] By Arrigo Boito.

Non ho più scritto aven=
do avuto la mia signora mala=
ta, la quale ha dovuto partire
per Napoli onde subire un'ope=
razione - Mentre scrivo è per=

WASHINGTON & BOWLING GREEN BLDGS
NEW YORK.

starcene - Tanti saluti
G. Simonelli

Arthur Strauss, Inc., Publishers, New York No. 159.

"I did not write anymore because my wife was ill, she had to leave for Naples to undergo surgery - As I am writing she is about to arrive in the port. Best regards

G. Simonelli"

PRIVATE MAILING CARD.
Authorized by Act of Congress of May 19th, 1898.
(POSTAL CARD—CARTE POSTALE.)

NEW YORK MAY 31 10 PM

Sig.r Enrico Cav Caruso
Tenore
Italy
Via Velasco N° 1
Milano

THIS SIDE IS EXCLUSIVELY FOR THE ADDRESS.

Egregio Sig.r
Caruso,
Non ho avuto più
sue buone nuove.
Il mio nuovo
indirizzo è
N° 9 Charlton St
New York
Tanti saluti
G Simonelli

SOUTH STREET AND BROOKLYN BRIDGE, NEW YORK.

"Distinguished Mr. Caruso, I did not receive any news from you - My new address is N. 9 Charlton St. New York
Many greetings G Simonelli"

***

A postcard mailed by Caruso from New York on May 16, 1903 to Giovanni, shows the relaxed tone they had become comfortable with. On the postcard there is a caricature that the tenor made of himself

"Dear Giovanni, Thank you for your letter. I am writing briefly because I am sleepy and I am going to sleep. Greetings your Caruso."

On June 26, 1904 Caruso writes a letter to Giovanni from the Hotel Cecil, Strand W.C., London.

HOTEL CECIL.
STRAND. W. C.

TELEPHONE No. 4682 GERRARD.
TELEGRAMS: "CECELIA, LONDON."

"6-26-904. Dear Giovanni, above all happy wishes for your name-day, a bit late but it is better late than never.[35] A thousand thanks for your words on my behalf that I accept very willingly. Greetings and best regards to your kind wife as I also beg you to extend my regards to Erziario[36] and Misses

[35] In Italy the name-day is celebrated as much as the birthday. According to the Catholic calendar of Saints, the day dedicated to Saint John the Baptist is June 24th.

[36] The five stars Restaurant Caruso, in Piazza Tasso - Sorrento

and to all your brothers[37] *and spouses. Embracing you, your ECaruso."*

On May 4th, 1905, Caruso sent a postcard to both P.[asquale] and G.[iovanni] from Cherbourg, department of Manche in the region of Lower Normandy, France. The card was numbered III, we are missing number I and II.

(Province of Naples), sports the tenor's memorabilia, including a letter of Erziario Simonelli to the singer.

[37] Twelve (including Pasquale, one sister and half-brother Giacomo).

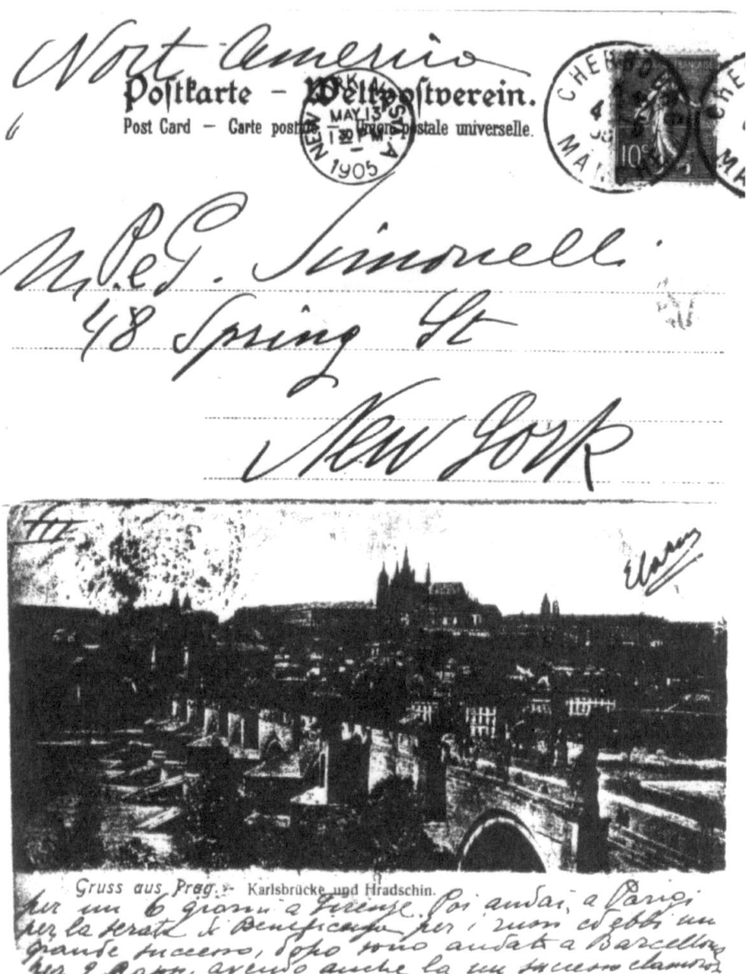

"... for about 6 days in Florence. Then I went to Paris for a charity evening for Russians and I had a great success, after I went to Barcelona for 2 performances, having even there a clamorous success... ECaruso."

Furthermore, a postcard mailed by Caruso from London on July 17, 1905 to Giovanni in Naples, Italy, expresses the tenor's sincere wish to meet him in Florence where Caruso was going to go on his return from London.

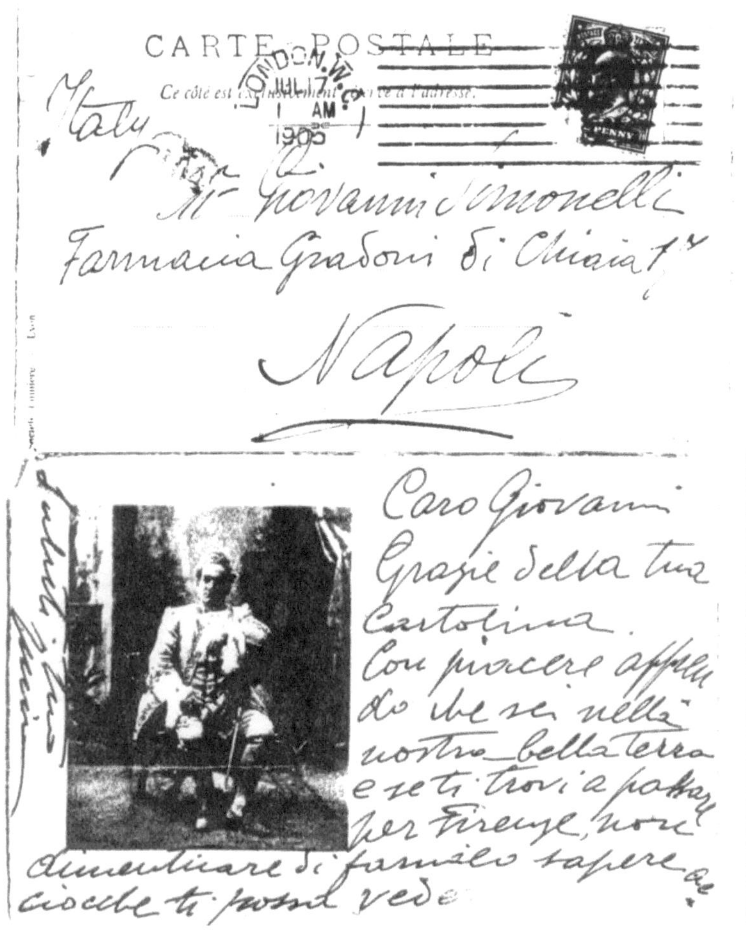

CARTE POSTALE

Ce côté est exclusivement réservé à l'adresse.

LONDON W.C. JUL 17 AM 1905

Italy

Giovanni Simonelli

Farmacia Gradoni di Chiaia 17

Napoli

Caro Giovanni
Grazie della tua
Cartolina.
Con piacere apprendo che sei nella
nostra bella terra
e se ti trovi a passare
per Firenze, non
dimenticare di farmelo sapere
acciocché ti possa vedere.

Saluti tuo Enrico

"Dear Giovanni. Thank you for your postcard With pleasure I understand that you are in our beautiful land and if you happen to go through Florence do not forget to let me know so I can see you. Regards your Enrico."

Eventually, Caruso went to visit Giovanni in Naples, as he describes in a letter to his brother Pasquale from his Villa Le Panche, Castello, (P. Firenze) .

VILLA LE PANCHE,
CASTELLO.
(P. FIRENZE).

Carissimo D. Pasqualino.

....

Fui a Napoli per pochi giorni e vidi Giovanni col quale passai molte belle ore. Peccato che parti senza vederlo perche partii all'improvviso. Chi sa cosa avrà pensato perche non mi ha scritto neanche un motto. Io volevo scrivergli ma non mi ricordo per dove indirizzare lo scritto. Ah! Adesso che ci penso scriverò ad un mio amico pregandolo di consegnare a Giovanni quello che gli vado a scrivere. . . . . . .

"Very Dear Don Pasqualino...
I was in Naples for a few days and I saw Giovanni with whom I spent many lovely hours. Too bad I left without seeing him because I left suddenly. I wonder what he thought because he did not write to me a line. I wanted to write to him but I do not

remember anymore where to mail the letter. Oh! Now that I think of it I will write to a friend of mine asking him to deliver to Giovanni that which I am about to write."

***

Caruso had a permanent residence at the Hotel Excelsior in Sorrento (province of Naples) Italy. To this day, his royal suite, with a huge terrace overlooking the Gulf of Naples, is named after him. However, it was at the Hotel Vesuvio, in Naples, that Caruso died on August 2, 1921, he was 48 years old. Among his casket bearers was Giovanni, faithful to his old friend Enrico until the end.

***

Eventually, Giovanni retired to San Paolo Belsito, province of Naples, Italy, where he, together with his brother Pasquale, had purchased a Villa.

There he spent the last part of his life.

***

On July 1905, from his Villa Le Panche, in Castello (Province of Florence), Caruso wrote to Pasquale about his daily activity,

Io lavoro sempre nel mio gran
casolare dove vi è sempre da
fare. Adesso ho incominciato a
modellare una testa intera del
mio Fofò e spero mi verrà bene.

"...I always work in my huge cottage where there is always something to do. Now I started to model an entire head of my Fofò [38] *and I hope it will turn out well..."*

Upon reading that, Pasquale requested Caruso for that sculpture to adorn the Villa he had purchased with Giovanni. On August 13, 1905, the tenor replied

Mi volete canzonare nel dire
che sperate il busto fatto da
me. Io non posso fare che
dei scarabocchi e che gli amici
gentili trovano che sono cose belle
invece io conosco che sono
delle piccole cose da chi vuol pas
sare il tempo perso; in quella
vostra villa vi metteremo una
fotografia e non un busto.

"... You want to tease me saying that you would like to have the bust made by me! I cannot do but scribblings,[39] *which gentle friends find them beautiful. Instead I know that they are little things done by someone who wants to kill time; in that villa of yours we will put a photograph and not a bust..."*

---

[38] Rodolfo (Fofò), his oldest son.

[39] He refers to his hobby as a caricaturist.

Giovanni's and Pasquale's Villa Simonelli

CHAPTER 2
The engagement at the Metropolitan Opera of New York

When Giovanni's postcards correspondence with Enrico Caruso ended, it was continued by his younger brother Pasquale Isidoro Simonelli.[40]

Pasquale left Naples, Italy at the age of 18 on the ship Oregon.[41] He arrived in New York City on February 10, 1897. He became an Italian-American banker, President of the Italian Savings Bank (1921)[42] and Vice-President of the East River Savings Bank, New York.[43] Victor Emmanuel III, King of Italy, conferred upon him the honor of *Commendatore*, Commander of the Order of the Crown of Italy. Throughout his life, Pasquale I. Simonelli engaged famous opera singers, such as Maria Barrientos, Beniamino Gigli, Titta Ruffo, Riccardo Stracciari, and others with the New York Metropolitan Opera. "In 1903, he was instrumental in securing the services of Enrico Caruso"[44] with that opera company.

---

[40] (1878-1960) *The Statue of Liberty-Ellis Island Foundation, Inc.*_# P00320-5 p. 182, line 0204. *Cf. Italian-American Who's-Who,* pp. 266-267.

[41] ID 82874.

[42] Italian Savings Bank, (1920?), *Italian Savings Bank. Chartered*

[43] Campbell Dorcas, *The First Hundred Years. The Chronicle of a Mutual Savings Bank*, pp. 67-69, 94.

[44] *Wikipedia* Pasquale I. Simonelli. *Cf.* Cannistraro ..., *Il Mattino* ... and *Il Progresso* ...

Pasquale I. Simonelli, New York City, September 22, 1935.

ITALIAN SAVINGS BANK

Main Offices, Spring Street, New York City

N°48 (1896-) N°64 (-1906-) N°60 (-1925-)

On August 7th, 1902, Pasquale informed Caruso that his engagement with the Metropolitan Opera House in New York City was off the table.

On August 25th, very surprised, Caruso replied, on letter head of the

"THEATRICAL AGENCY G. ARGENTI & COMP. - DIRECTION OF THE PERIODICAL *LA LANTERNA*,"

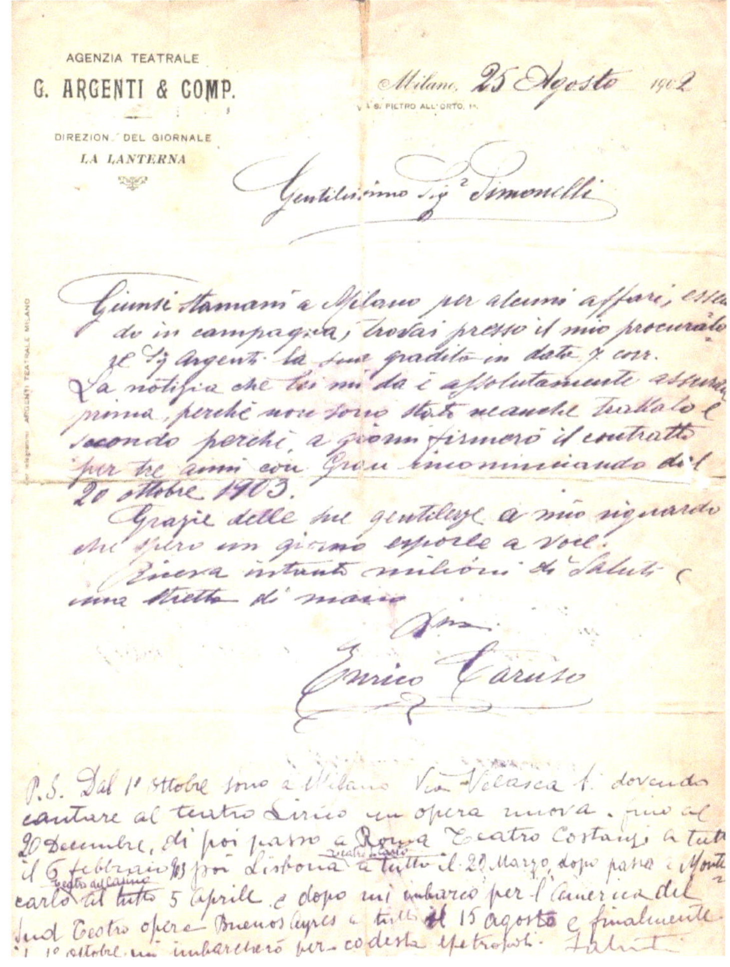

AGENZIA TEATRALE
G. ARGENTI & COMP.
DIREZION. DEL GIORNALE
LA LANTERNA

Milano, 25 Agosto 1902
V. S. Pietro all'Orto, 1.

Gentilissimo Sig.r Simonelli

Giunsi stamani a Milano per alcuni affari, essendo in campagna, trovai presso il mio procuratore il Sig. Argenti la sua gradita in data 7 corr.
La notizia che lei mi dà è assolutamente assurda prima, perchè non sono stato neanche trattato e secondo perchè, a giorni firmerò il contratto per tre anni con Grau incominciando dal 20 ottobre 1903.
Grazie delle sue gentilezze a mio riguardo che spero un giorno esporle a voce.
Riceva intanto milioni di saluti e una stretta di mano

Suo
Enrico Caruso

P.S. Dal 1° ottobre sono a Milano Via Velasca 1. dovendo cantare al teatro Lirico un opera nuova, fino al 20 Decembre, di poi passo a Roma Teatro Costanzi a tutto il 6 febbraio 903 poi Lisbona teatro San Carlo a tutto il 20 Marzo, dopo passo a Monte Carlo teatro del Casino a tutto 5 aprile e dopo mi imbarco per l'America del Sud Teatro Opera Buenos Ayres a tutto il 15 agosto e finalmente il 1° ottobre mi imbarcherò per codesta Metropoli. Saluti

"Very kind Mr. Simonelli
I arrived this morning at Milano for some business, having been in the countryside, I found with my procurator Mr. Argenti your welcomed letter dated August 7th.
The news that you give me is absolutely absurd first, because I was not even consulted and second

because within days I will be signing a three year contract with Grau[45] *starting from October 3, 1903. Thank you for your kindness towards me that I hope one day to express directly.*
In the meanwhile receive a million greetings and a handshake.
Yours Enrico Caruso
P.S. From October 1st I will be in Milano Via Velasca 1 having to sing a new opera at the Theater Lirico until December 20th after which I will go to Rome Theater Costanzo until February 6th 1903 then Lisbon Theater de Carlo until March 20th after which I will depart for South America the Opera Theater of Buenos Aires until August 15th and finally October 1st I will depart for this Metropolis [NYC]. Greetings."

Caruso did not know yet, but he was soon to find out that his contract with Grau was off the table.

> Pasquale remembered,
> "On January 30, 1903, my brother John [Giovanni] received a letter from Caruso dated from Rome. In it he wrote that Maurice Grau had informed him that he was sorry to have to dissolve the contract made, as he would not continue to be the general manager of the Metropolitan Opera House... Caruso asked my brother if he would communicate with the Metropolitan's new manager in an endeavor to see what might be done. My brother John was so occupied with his own affairs that he

---

[45] Maurice Grau, President and Managing Director of the Metropolitan Opera House of New York City.

charged me to undertake the commission. When, on February 19, 1903, newspapers announcements informed the public that Heinrich Conried had been appointed to the management of the Metropolitan, I went that very afternoon to see him in his office at the Irving Place Theater of which he was then director."[46]

Pasquale went to Conried with a phonograph and a record of Caruso singing *Vesti la giubba*.[47] At the time gramophones were not common household items. In later years, recalling the event, he was heard saying what an ordeal it was to get in and out of the cab with that cumbersome turntable.

Upon hearing Caruso's recorded voice, Conried remarked, "If that Caruso can sing as well in the Metropolitan as he sang to make that record… his success is assured."[48]

After speaking with Conried, Pasquale, seeking to secure also Grau's support, wrote the following letter to him at 49 W. 56th St. NYC.

---

[46] Key, *Enrico Caruso a biography*, pp. 170-171.

[47] Caruso, Salvatore Cottone, piano, Recorded in Milan, 30th November 1902. (Put on the costume) end of Act 1 from Leoncavallo's *Pagliacci*. In 1904 Caruso will be selling one million (first in history) records of this aria.

[48] Key, *Enrico Caruso a biography*, p. 181.

Maurice Grau Esq.

Dear Sir

I called to see you at the Met. Op Ho. at the suggestion of Mr Caruso from whom I received a letter authorizing me to confer with you about the contract for for performances in this country. I was referred by one of the managers at the Metrop. Op H to your successor, Mr. Conried, upon the subject -

I had a conversation with Mr. Conried and stated to him the fact of your having a contract with Mr Caruso - Mr Conried stated that the Contract was cancelled and that he himself had never heard Mr Caruso but that he would enter into an engagement for 20 performances with Mr Caruso and at the end of the last performance of the third week he would inform Mr. Caruso as to whether or not he would extend the contract to the whole season or 40 performances. I immediately called this state of affairs to Mr Caruso -

I take the liberty, now, of writing to you upon this subject as you are the well-known musical impresario of this Country and your successor Mr. Conried would naturally rely upon your judgment in making a contract with such an artist.

I submit to you that Mr. Caruso is an artist of such ability and renown that it is not necessary for him to be heard to be appreciated. His fame is a sufficient guarantee of his value and it is not a question of his success as that is assured but of being able to engage the services of such a meritorious artist -

I have to request that you write to Mr. Conried unfolding this views as to the musical standing and great merit of Mr Caruso, as I know that coming from you Mr. Conried will waive the question of his personally hearing Mr. Caruso and rely upon his well-known artistic ability and your appreciation of it -

I trust I am not intruding upon your time in this matter but knowing your great interest in making a success

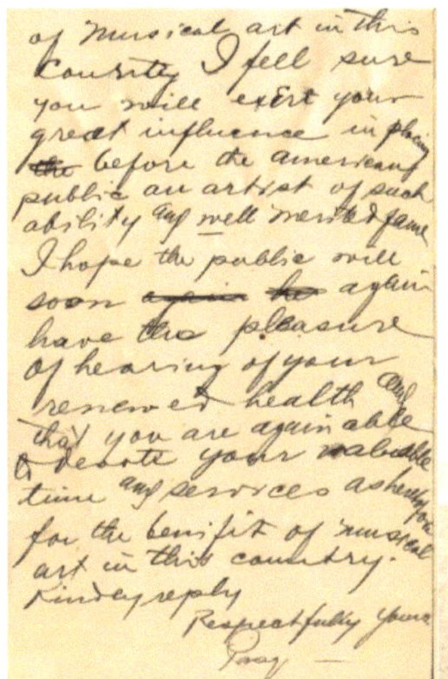

of musical art in this country I feel sure you will exert your great influence in placing ~~the~~ before the american public an artist of such ability and well merited fame. I hope the public will soon ~~again~~ ~~to~~ again have the pleasure of hearing of your renewed health and that you are again able to devote your valuable time and services as heretofore for the benefit of musical art in this country. Kindly reply

Respectfully yours

Pasq —

ITALIAN SAVINGS BANK
CLEVELAND SQUARE
COR. SPRING & LAFAYETTE STS.
NEW YORK

Original rough draft of Simonelli's letter to Grau

"Maurice Grau Esq.
Dear Sir
I called to see you at the Metropolitan Opera House at the suggestion of Mr. Caruso from whom I received a letter authorizing me to confer with you about the Contract for performances in this country. I was referred by one of the Managers at the Metropolitan Opera House to your successor Mr. Conried, upon the subject -
I had a conversation with Mr. Conried and stated to him the fact of your having a contract with Mr. Caruso -
Mr. Conried stated that the Contract was cancelled and that he - himself had never heard Mr. Caruso but that he would enter into an engagement for 20 performances with Mr. Caruso and at the end of the last performance of the Third week he would inform Mr. Caruso as to whether or not he would extend the contract to the whole season on 40 performances I

immediately cabled this state of affairs to Mr. Caruso-
I take the liberty, now, of writing to you upon this subject as you are the well-known musical impresario of this Country and your successor Mr. Conried would naturally rely upon your judgment in making a contract with such an artist.
I submit to you that Mr. Caruso is an artist of such ability and renown that it is not necessary for him to be heard to be appreciated. His fame is a sufficient guarantee of his value and it is not a question of his success as that is assured but of being able to engage the services of such a meritorious artist -
I have to request that you write to Mr. Conried unfolding this views as to the musical standing and great merit of Mr. Caruso, as I know that coming from you Mr. Conried will waive the question of his personally hearing Mr. Caruso and rely upon his well-known artistic ability and your appreciation of it -
I trust I am not intruding upon your time in this matter but knowing your great interest in making a success of Musical art in this Country I feel sure you will exert your great influence in placing before the American public an artist of such ability and well merited fame. I hope the public will soon again have the pleasure of hearing of your renewed health and that you are again able to devote your valuable time and services as heretofore for the benefit of musical art in this country -
Kindly reply
Respectfully yours
Pasquale Simonelli"

Maurice Grau Opera Co.
Lessees and Managers of
The Metropolitan Opera House

New York Feb. 25, 1903.

Pasquale I. Simonelli, Esq,
Sec'y Italian Savings Bank,
43 Spring Street, City

Dear sir-

Mr. Grau desires me to say in reply to your favor of Feb. 24th, that in the matter of the engagement of Mr. Caruso, he can only refer you to his successor, Mr. Conried, as he himself is compelled by his illness, to abstain from attending to any business at present.

Yours very truly,

Secretary

Reply of Grau's secretary

Ernest Goerlitz, Grau's Secretary, replied on February 25th. He stated that his boss' health condition prevented him to be of any help in the matter. Therefore, he directed Simonelli to Conried.

Thus, Grau missed the historical opportunity to engage Caruso.

The same day Simonelli, after seeing Conried, wired Caruso in Lisbon,

POSTAL TELEGRAPH-CABLE COMPANY IN CONNECTION WITH THE COMMERCIAL CABLE COMPANY.

CLARENCE H. MACKAY, President. J. O. STEVENS, Sec'y. WM. H. BAKER, V. P. & G. M.

CLARENCE H. MACKAY, President. ALBERT BECK, Sec'y. GEO. G. WARD, V. P. & G. M.

TELEGRAM

The Postal Telegraph-Cable Company transmits and delivers this message subject to the terms and conditions printed on the back of this blank.

Counter Number.	Time Filed.	Check
	M.	20 — $7 80

Send the following message, without repeating, subject to the terms and conditions printed on the back hereof, which are hereby agreed to.

To Tenore Caruso Feb 19 1903

Lisbona

Nuovo impresario accetterebbe contratto Grau riducendo primo anno metà recite tempo relativo vostro successo prolungherebbe ~~contratto~~ recite

Simonelli

THE POSTAL COMPANY'S SYSTEM REACHES ALL IMPORTANT POINTS IN THE UNITED STATES AND BRITISH AMERICA, AND via COMMERCIAL CABLES, ALL THE WORLD.

OFFICE. FEB 20 1903

190

RECEIVED $ Seven 80/100

for Message to Tenore Caruso

Lisbon

A H H Receiver.

"February 19 1903 Tenor Caruso Lisbon
New impresario would accept Grau's contract reducing first year time half performances relative to your success would prolong performances. Simonelli"

Following his telegram, Pasquale wrote to Caruso explaining with more details the reasons why he should accept Conried's contract. Here are selected excerpts from a rough draft of that letter,

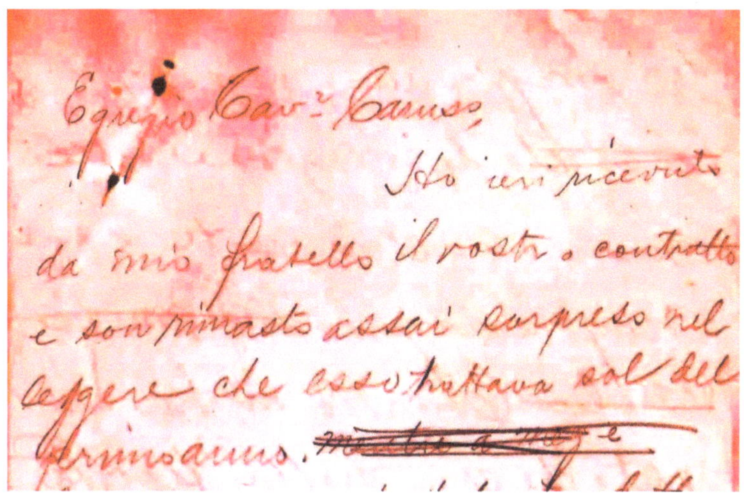

Egregio Cav. Caruso,
Ho ieri ricevuto da mio fratello il vostro contratto e son rimasto assai sorpreso nel leggere che esso trattava sol del primo anno.

"Very distinguished Chevalier Caruso,
I received from my brother your contract and I was very surprised reading that it dealt only with the first year..."

Conried insiste intero contratto Grau riserbando dritto ridurre, solo primo anno, numero recite

"...Conried insists on the entire Grau's contract, only reserving the right of reducing, for the first year, the number of performances...

a venticinque - non meno di due recite settimanali cominciando ventitre Novembre Deposito anticipo sarà eseguito data Dovreste telegrafarmi accettanza Conried siccome rimane impegnato solo fino a martedì

to twenty five. Not less than two performances per week starting November twenty three. The anticipated deposit will be executed on the date. You should

<u>telegraph me your acceptance since Conried will hold the deal only until Tuesday</u>..."

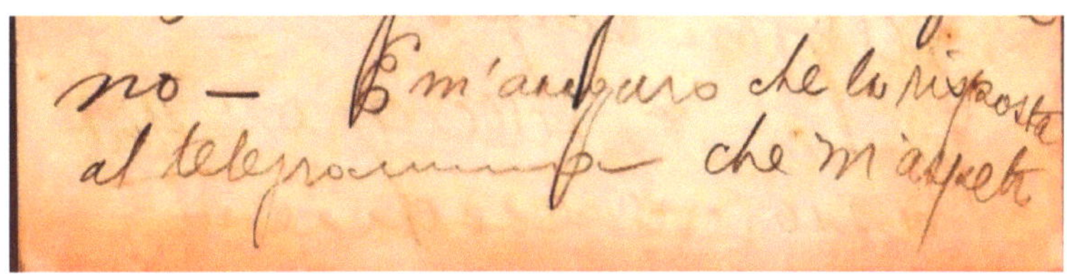

no — E m'auguro che la risposta
al telegramma che m'aspetto

"I hope that the answer to the telegram I'm waiting for..."

da voi per stasera o domattina
sarà affermativa -
Me l'auguro per voi perchè

"... from you tonight or tomorrow night will be affirmative. I wish it for you because..."

dei milliardari fareste
il vostro miglior guada-
gno - Me l'auguro perchè

"... You would make the best gain. - I wish it also because..."

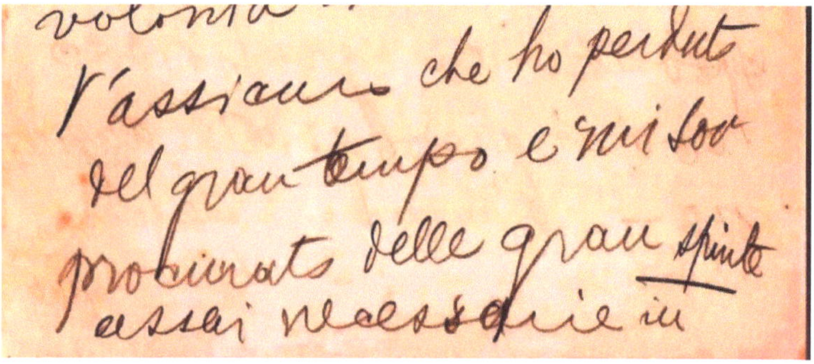

volontà
l'assicuro che ho perduto
del gran tempo e mi son
procurato delle gran spinte
assai necessarie in

"I assure you that I spent a lot of time and I procured many pushes very necessary in..."

questo paese Sommo per
la gran mole degli affari —
Io nulla ho tralasciato son
ricorso a Grau ai rap-
presentanti di Conried ed agli
artisti stessi qui per ottenere
che essi parlassero a Conried
con quell'ammirazione degna
della vostra grand'arte
e solo così ho ottenuto il
sopravvento su Bongi che
si offriva ad assai più fa-
vorevoli condizioni anche
lui conosciuto qui per bella

"... this country, the greatest for the great quantity of businesses. I left nothing undone. I went to Grau, to Conried's representatives and to the artists themselves so that they would talk to Conried with that admiration worthy of your great art and only this way I obtained the upper hand over Bonci who offered himself at a much more favorable conditions he was also known here for his beautiful..."

fama = Vi dirò anche
che altri prima di me e
da Milano aveva trattata
la vostra scrittura col
Conried ma senza alcun
successo sicchè voi non dovete
costì commissione ad
alcuno poichè chi vi scrittura
se tutto finirà bene, sono
io e nessun altro —

"... fame = I will tell you also that others before me and from Milan had tried to get your engagement with Conried but without any success therefore you owe no commission to anyone because who engages you if all will end well is I and no one else.----"

In fact, Pasquale Simonelli was the only one who successfully convinced Conried to engage Caruso in place of his choice of the tenor Alessandro Bonci.[49]

Later, on June, 1903, first from Florence and then from Buenos Aires, Caruso, on the issue of Bonci, made these remarks,

Dell'affare Bonci io non c'entro per nulla prima perchè non faccio il comodo di nessuno e poi perchè ho deciso di starmene tranquillo, anzi a questo proposito feci smentire dalla Tribuna tutte le chiacchiere che si facevano.

"... I have nothing to do with the Bonci business, first because I do not as other like and then I have decided to be tranquil. Actually, on this issue I had the Tribuna[50] stop all the gossip."

From Buenos Aires Caruso was more esplicit,

[49] Tenor Alessandro Bonci was born at Cesana, Italy in 1870.

[50] *La Tribuna*, a Roman daily newspaper.

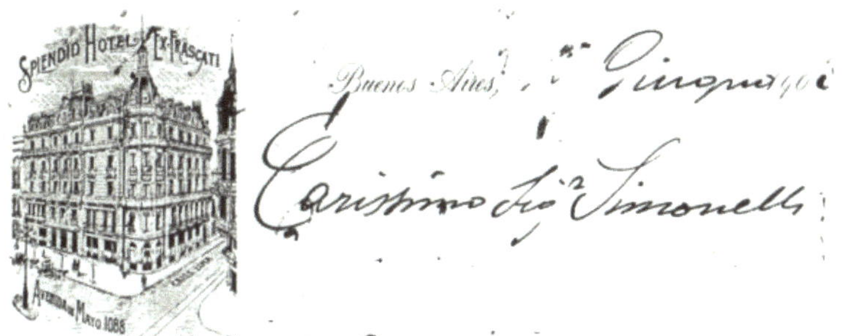
Splendid Hotel Ex-Frascati
Avenida de Mayo 1086
Buenos Aires, 1° Giugno 903

Carissimo Sig.r Simonelli

....

Non vi nascondo che non vedo di buon occhio la scrittura di Bonci non già che mi faccia paura come artista perchè io son Caruso e lui è Bonci e tra noi vi è un abbisso, ma come uomo non è una buona parte. Spero che il suo contratto sia dopo il mio, perciò pregovi informarmene..

....

Una volta scritturato il Bonci vedete se [illegible] potete far [illegible] del Barbiere, Don Pasquale, Nozze di Figaro e Flauto Magico perchè è troppo lavoro per imparare tutte ciò pel primo anno mentre potrò farle il secondo, se a questi [illegible] andrò a genio.

"June 1903. Very Dear Mr. Simonelli...

...I am not hiding from you that I do not appreciate the engagement of Bonci, not because I am afraid of him as an artist, because I am Caruso he is Bonci and between us there is an

abyss, but as a man he is not good stuff. I hope his engagement will be after mine, therefore please keep me posted...
... Once Bonci is engaged see if I can get rid of the Barbiere; Don Pasquale; Nozze di Figaro and Flauto Magico;[51] *because it is too much work to learn all those next year, when I could do them the second year if those gentlemen will find me agreeable...*"

However, before writing those letters, Caruso had replied from Lisbon, on February 22, 1903, to Pasquale's telegram.

[51] *Il barbiere di Siviglia* (Rossini), *Don Pasquale* (Donizetti), *Le nozze di Figaro* and *Il flauto Magico* (both by Mozart).

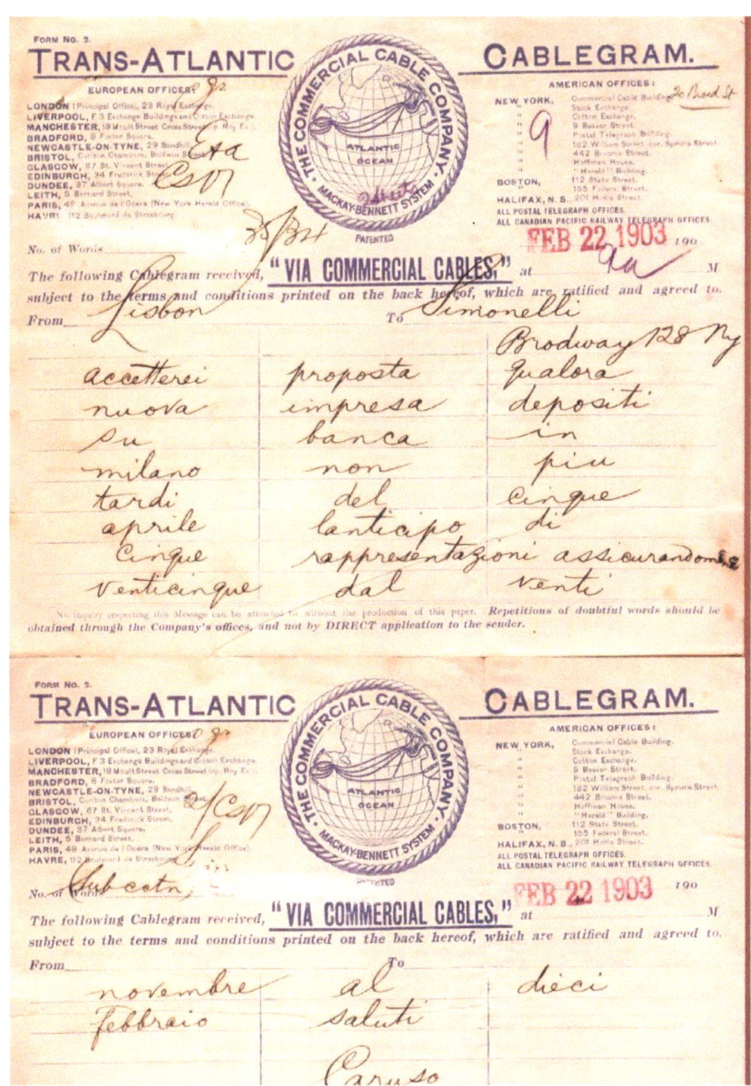

FORM No. 2.

TRANS-ATLANTIC CABLEGRAM.

THE COMMERCIAL CABLE COMPANY. ATLANTIC OCEAN. MACKAY-BENNETT SYSTEM. PATENTED

EUROPEAN OFFICES:
LONDON (Principal Office), 23 Royal Exchange.
LIVERPOOL, F 3 Exchange Buildings and Cotton Exchange.
MANCHESTER, 18 Moult Street, Cross Street.
BRADFORD, 8 Foster Square.
NEWCASTLE-ON-TYNE, 29 Sandhill.
BRISTOL, Cotton Chambers, Baldwin Street.
GLASGOW, 67 St. Vincent Street.
EDINBURGH, 34 Frederick Street.
DUNDEE, 37 Albert Square.
LEITH, 5 Bernard Street.
PARIS, 49 Avenue de l'Opera (New York Herald Office).
HAVRE, 112 Boulevard de Strasbourg.

AMERICAN OFFICES:
NEW YORK, Commercial Cable Building, 20 Broad St.
Stock Exchange.
Cotton Exchange.
9 Beaver Street.
Postal Telegraph Building.
182 William Street, cor. Spruce Street.
442 Broome Street.
Hoffman House.
"Herald" Building.
BOSTON, 112 State Street.
155 Federal Street.
HALIFAX, N. S., 201 Hollis Street.
ALL POSTAL TELEGRAPH OFFICES.
ALL CANADIAN PACIFIC RAILWAY TELEGRAPH OFFICES.

No. of Words 9 Eta CSV 1 35/B24

FEB 22 1903 190 9a M

The following Cablegram received, "VIA COMMERCIAL CABLES," at ... M
subject to the terms and conditions printed on the back hereof, which are ratified and agreed to.

From Lisbon To Simonelli Broadway 128 Ny

accetterei proposta qualora
nuova impresa depositi
su banca in
milano non piu
tardi del cinque
aprile lanticipo di
cinque rappresentazioni assicurandomi
venticinque dal venti

No inquiry respecting this Message can be attended to without the production of this paper. Repetitions of doubtful words should be obtained through the Company's offices, and not by DIRECT application to the sender.

FORM No. 2.

TRANS-ATLANTIC CABLEGRAM.

No. of Words 2/CSV Subcotn

FEB 22 1903 190

The following Cablegram received, "VIA COMMERCIAL CABLES," at ... M
subject to the terms and conditions printed on the back hereof, which are ratified and agreed to.

From ... To

novembre al dieci
febbraio saluti
Caruso

"From Lisbon to Simonelli Broadway 128 NY
I would accept proposal if new impresario would deposit on bank in Milan not later than April fifth down payment for five performances assuring me twenty-five from November twentieth to February tenth greetings Caruso."

HE WESTERN UNION TELEGRAPH COMPANY.
INCORPORATED
21,000 OFFICES IN AMERICA. CABLE SERVICE TO ALL THE WORLD.
THOS. T. ECKERT, President and General Manager.

Receiver's No. Time Filed Check

SEND the following message subject to the terms on back hereof, which are hereby agreed to.

CABLE 190

To Caruso - Lisbon -

Conried insiste intiero contratto Grau riservandosi dritto ridurre primo anno numero recite venticinque - non meno di due recite settimanali cominciando ventitre Novembre Deposito anticipo sarà eseguito pel cinque Aprile Dovreste telegrafarmi accettanza siccome Conried rimane impegnato solo fino a martedì.

Simonelli

IRVING PLACE THEATRE

READ THE NOTICE AND AGREEMENT ON BACK.

Simonelli replied to Caruso in Lisbon

"To Caruso Lisbon. Conried insists on the entire Grau contract reserving the right to reduce for the first year number of performances to twenty five and not less than two performances a week starting on the twenty third of November. An anticipated down payment will be done on April fifth. You should wire me your acceptance since Conried will be bounded to this contract only until Tuesday. Simonelli."

FORM No. 2.

TRANS-ATLANTIC CABLEGRAM.

THE COMMERCIAL CABLE COMPANY. ATLANTIC OCEAN. MACKAY-BENNETT SYSTEM. PATENTED

EUROPEAN OFFICES: LONDON (Principal Office), 23 Royal Exchange. LIVERPOOL, F 3 Exchange Buildings and Cotton Exchange. MANCHESTER, 18 Moult Street Cross Street (op. Roy. Ex.). BRADFORD, 8 Foster Square. NEWCASTLE-ON-TYNE, 29 Sandhill. BRISTOL, Carlton Chambers, Baldwin Street. GLASGOW, 67 St. Vincent Street. EDINBURGH, 34 Frederick Street. DUNDEE, 4 Albert Square. LEITH, 6 Bernard Street. PARIS, 49 Avenue de l'Opera (New York Herald Office). HAVRE, 112 Boulevard de Strasbourg.

AMERICAN OFFICES: NEW YORK, Commercial Cable Building. Stock Exchange. Cotton Exchange. 9 Beaver Street. Postal Telegraph Building. 182 William Street, cor. Spruce Street. 442 Broome Street. Hoffman House. "Herald" Building. BOSTON, 112 State Street. 156 Federal Street. HALIFAX, N. S., 201 Hollis Street. ALL POSTAL TELEGRAPH OFFICES. ALL CANADIAN PACIFIC RAILWAY TELEGRAPH OFFICES.

No. of Words 40 — MAR 15 1903 190

The following Cablegram received, **"VIA COMMERCIAL CABLES,"** at 12.... M. subject to the terms and conditions printed on the back hereof, which are ratified and agreed to.

From Lisbon To Simonelli Broadway 128 NY

Accetto intiero Contratto grau riserbandosi Conried ridurre per il primo anno le recite a venticinque non meno di due per settimana

No inquiry respecting this Message can be attended to without the production of this paper. Repetitions of doubtful words should be obtained through the Company's offices, and not by DIRECT application to the sender.

The following Cablegram received, "VIA COMMERCIAL CABLES" subject to the terms and conditions printed on the back hereof, which are ratified and agreed to.

From To

Cominciando venticinque Novembre il presente vale come contratto in attesa benestare Conried qui amicizie Caruso

Form 54. THE COMMERCIAL CABLE COMPANY. PATENTED

OFFICE. MAR 16 1903 190

RECEIVED, $ 3 90/

for Message to Caruso Lisbon

Caruso answered on March 15th and receipt 3/16/1903. "From Lisbon to Simonelli. I accept the entire contract Grau while Conried reserves the right to reduce the first year the performances to twenty five not less than two per week starting November twenty fifth the present is valid as contract expecting Conried's acceptance. Friendship Caruso."

HE POSTAL COMPANY'S SYSTEM REACHES ALL IMPORTANT POINTS IN THE UNITED STATES AND BRITISH AMERICA, AND via COMMERCIAL CABLES, TO ALL THE WORLD.

5.—Books.

TELEGRAM

All Messages taken by this Company are subject to the conditions printed on the back of this Blank.

ALBERT B. CHANDLER, President and General Manager. JOHN O. STEVENS, Secretary.

Send the following Message, without repeating, subject to the conditions printed on the back hereof, which are hereby agreed to.

"CABLE" 189

To Caruso
Lisbon

Contratto chiuso- Pagheretemi
tre percento commissione
Felicitazioni Simonelli

Simonelli, triumphant, cables Caruso in Lisboan on 3/16/1903.

"Contract completed. You will pay me three percent commission. Congratulations Simonelli."

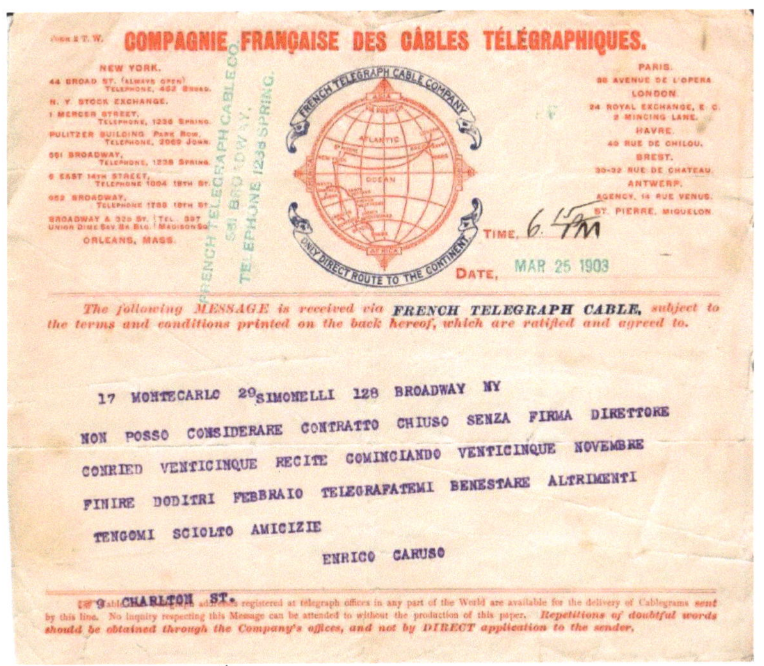

COMPAGNIE FRANÇAISE DES CÂBLES TÉLÉGRAPHIQUES.

NEW YORK.
44 BROAD ST. (ALWAYS OPEN) TELEPHONE, 462 BROAD.
N. Y. STOCK EXCHANGE.
1 MERCER STREET, TELEPHONE, 1236 SPRING.
PULITZER BUILDING PARK ROW, TELEPHONE, 2069 JOHN.
561 BROADWAY, TELEPHONE, 1238 SPRING.
6 EAST 14TH STREET, TELEPHONE 1004 18TH ST.
952 BROADWAY, TELEPHONE 1788 18TH ST.
BROADWAY & 32D ST. UNION DIME SAV. BK. BLG. TEL. 397 MADISON SQ.
ORLEANS, MASS.

FRENCH TELEGRAPH CABLE CO.
561 BROADWAY,
TELEPHONE 1238 SPRING.

FRENCH TELEGRAPH CABLE COMPANY
ONLY DIRECT ROUTE TO THE CONTINENT

PARIS.
38 AVENUE DE L'OPERA
LONDON.
24 ROYAL EXCHANGE, E. C.
2 MINCING LANE.
HAVRE.
40 RUE DE CHILOU.
BREST.
30-32 RUE DE CHATEAU.
ANTWERP.
AGENCY, 14 RUE VENUS.
ST. PIERRE, MIQUELON.

TIME, 6.45 PM

DATE, MAR 25 1903

The following MESSAGE is received via **FRENCH TELEGRAPH CABLE,** *subject to the terms and conditions printed on the back hereof, which are ratified and agreed to.*

17 MONTECARLO 29 SIMONELLI 128 BROADWAY NY
NON POSSO CONSIDERARE CONTRATTO CHIUSO SENZA FIRMA DIRETTORE
CONRIED VENTICINQUE RECITE COMINCIANDO VENTICINQUE NOVEMBRE
FINIRE DODITRI FEBBRAIO TELEGRAFATEMI BENESTARE ALTRIMENTI
TENGOMI SCIOLTO AMICIZIE
ENRICO CARUSO

9 CHARLTON ST.

Cable addresses registered at telegraph offices in any part of the World are available for the delivery of Cablegrams *sent* by this line. No inquiry respecting this Message can be attended to without the production of this paper. *Repetitions of doubtful words should be obtained through the Company's offices, and not by DIRECT application to the sender.*

On March 25th, 1903, Caruso replies from Montecarlo.

"17 Montecarlo 29. Simonelli Broadway NY. I cannot consider contract closed without the signature of Director Conried twenty five performances starting November twenty fifth ending February twelve. Wire me acceptance if not I will consider myself free from obligations. Friendship Enrico Caruso."

Form No. 2.

THE WESTERN UNION TELEGRAPH COMPANY.

INCORPORATED

23,000 OFFICES IN AMERICA. CABLE SERVICE TO ALL THE WORLD.

ROBERT C. CLOWRY, President and General Manager.

Receiver's No.	Time Filed	Check

SEND the following message subject to the terms on back hereof, which are hereby agreed to. Mar 25th 1903

To Caruso

Montecarlo.

Spediscovi Milano contratto firmato Conried. Troverretevi vostri interessi intieramente, legalmente cautelati.

Simonelli

READ THE NOTICE AND AGREEMENT ON BACK.

Form No. 2.

THE WESTERN UNION TELEGRAPH COMPANY.

INCORPORATED

23,000 OFFICES IN AMERICA. CABLE SERVICE TO ALL THE WORLD.

ROBERT C. CLOWRY, President and General Manager.

Receiver's No.	Time Filed	Check

SEND the following message subject to the terms on back hereof, which are hereby agreed to. 190

To

Rec'd $3,50 Montecarlo Cable

599 Broadway MAR 25 1903

G3W

READ THE NOTICE AND AGREEMENT ON BACK.

Simonelli answers on March 25th, 1903 with receipt.

"March 25th, 1903. To Caruso Montecarlo. I will send you the contract signed Conried. In it you will find all your interests legally protected. Simonelli."

COMPAGNIE FRANÇAISE DES CÂBLES TÉLÉGRAPHIQUES.

NEW YORK.
44 BROAD ST. (ALWAYS OPEN) TELEPHONE, 452 BROAD.
N. Y. STOCK EXCHANGE.
1 MERCER STREET, TELEPHONE, 1238 SPRING.
PULITZER BUILDING PARK ROW. TELEPHONE, 2069 JOHN
561 BROADWAY, TELEPHONE, 1238 SPRING.
5 EAST 14TH STREET, TELEPHONE 1004 18TH ST.
952 BROADWAY, TELEPHONE 1708 18TH ST
BROADWAY & 22D ST. UNION DIME SAV. BK. BLD. TEL., 397 MADISON SQ.
ORLEANS, MASS.

FRENCH TELEGRAPH CABLE COMPANY
ONLY DIRECT ROUTE TO THE CONTINENT

PARIS.
38 AVENUE DE L'OPERA.
LONDON.
34 ROYAL EXCHANGE, E. C.
2 MINCING LANE.
HAVRE.
40 RUE DE CHILOU.
BREST.
30-32 RUE DE CHATEAU.
ANTWERP.
AGENCY, 14 RUE VENUS.
ST. PIERRE, MIQUELON.

TIME, 259

DATE, MAR 26 1903

The following MESSAGE is received via **FRENCH TELEGRAPH CABLE**, *subject to the terms and conditions printed on the back hereof, which are ratified and agreed to.*

B 561 MONTECARLO 47

SIMONELLI 128 BROADWAY NY

VOSTRO TELEGRAMMA NON RISPOND ALLE MIE DOMANDE FATEMI TELEGRAFARE FIRMATO CONRIED QUESTI TERMINI STA BENE VENTIC-INQUE RECITE COMINCIANDO VENTICINQUE NOVEMBRE PROSSIMO TERMINANDO DODICI FEBBRAIO 1904 RESTANDO ESATTAMENTE ALTRE CONDIZIONI CONTRATTO SPEDITOVI NON RICEVENDO ENTRO TRE GIORNI TALE TELEGRAMMA TENGOMI SCIOLTO OGNI IMPEGNO CARUSO

Cable and Telegraph addresses registered at telegraph offices in any part of the World are available for the delivery of Cablegrams *sent by this line.* No inquiry respecting this Message can be attended to without the production of this paper. *Repetitions of doubtful words should be obtained through the Company's offices, and not by DIRECT application to the sender.*

On March 26th, 1903, Caruso replies

"B 561 Montecarlo 47 Simonelli 128 Broadway NY. Your telegram does not answer my questions send me a telegram signed by Conried with the agreements that it is acceptable twenty five performances starting next November twenty fifth ending February twelve 1904 retaining exactly the other conditions of the contrast I sent you. If I do not receive such telegram within three days, I will consider myself free from any obligation. Caruso."

Form T. W.

COMPAGNIE FRANÇAISE DES CÂBLES TÉLÉGRAPHIQUES.

NEW YORK.
44 BROAD ST. (ALWAYS OPEN) TELEPHONE, 452 BROAD.
N. Y. STOCK EXCHANGE.
1 MERCER STREET, TELEPHONE, 1236 SPRING.
PULITZER BUILDING PARK ROW, TELEPHONE, 2069 JOHN.
581 BROADWAY, TELEPHONE, 1238 SPRING.
5 EAST 14TH STREET, TELEPHONE 1004 18TH ST.
952 BROADWAY, TELEPHONE 1788 18TH ST.
BROADWAY & 32D ST. UNION DIME SAV. BK. BLG. TEL., 397 MADISON SQ.
ORLEANS, MASS.

PARIS.
36 AVENUE DE L'OPERA.
LONDON.
24 ROYAL EXCHANGE, E. C.
2 MINCING LANE.
HAVRE.
40 RUE DE CHILOU.
BREST.
30-32 RUE DE CHATEAU.
ANTWERP.
AGENCY, 14 RUE VENUS.
ST. PIERRE, MIQUELON.

No. W'ds Ch'ge Via Time F. No. May 19 1903.

Send the following message, "VIA FRENCH," subject to the terms and conditions printed on the back hereof, which are agreed to.

Caruso

Buenos-Ayres-

Your conditions accepted

Conried

by authorization on telephone May 18th 1903. 10 30 o'clock

N. B.—Please send the Conditions and write your Name and Address on the back for reference.

Conried replied on May 19, 1903.

“Caruso Buenos Aires – Your conditions accepted. Conried.

By authorization on telephone May 18th – 1903 – 10:30 o’clock”

Rough draft of Caruso's contract

Colla presente scrittura fatta in doppio origi-
nale fra
e il Signor Cav: Uff: Enrico Caruso si conviene
quanto segue:
I° scrittura il Signor
Cav: Uff: Enrico Caruso dal 21 Novembre 1903
al 10 Febbraio 1904 incluso per fare uso dei suoi
talenti artistici nella qualità di primo
tenore assoluto
II° assicura al Signor Cav:
Uff: Enrico Caruso venticinque rappresentazioni dal 21 Novembre 1903 al 10 Febbraio 1904
III° Il Signor Cav: Uff: Enrico Caruso riceverà
il cachet di Franchi Cinquemila (fr 5.000)
e detta somma sarà consegnata non più
tardi delle ore tre pomeridiane del giorno
in cui deve eseguirsi la rappresentazione.
IV° a garanzia del contrat-
to depositerà alla Banca Commerciale in
Milano non più tardi del giorno cinque
Aprile 1903 l'anticipo di cinque rappresen-
tazioni pari a Franchi Venticinquemila (fr 25.000) che il Signor Cav: Uff: Enrico
Caruso potrà ritirare dieci giorni prima
della sua partenza dall'Europa. Detta
somma gli verrà poi trattenuta dalla
in parti uguali
di Mille franchi (fr 1000) su ciascuna delle venticinque rappresentazioni
V° accorda al

"With the following writing in two originals between ....
and Mr. Chevalier Enrico Caruso it is agreed as follows:

I- Chevalier Officer Enrico Caruso from

November 20th, 1903 to February 10th, 1904 included utilizing his artistic talents in the capacity of absolute first tenor

II- ....assures Mr. Chevalier Officer Enrico Caruso twenty five performances from November 20, 1903 to February 19, 1904.

III- Mr. Chevalier Officer Enrico Caruso will receive the cachet of five thousand Francs (Fr. 5,000) and such amount will be delivered not later than three o'clock p.m. of the day the performance takes place.

IV- .... to guarantee the contract will deposit at the Banca Commerciale in Milan not later than April fifth 1903 the down payment of five performances equivalent to Francs twenty five thousand (Fr. 25,000), which Mr. Chevalier Officer Enrico Caruso will be able to withdraw ten days before his departure from Europe. Such sum will then be withheld by .... in equal parts of one thousand Franks (Fr. 1,000) from each of the twenty five performances.

V- .... will grant"

Signor Cav: Uff: Enrico Caruso i viaggi pagati per tre persone in I^a Classe e due in II^a dall'Europa in America e viceversa e così pure i viaggi e bagagli occorrenti nella permanenza negli Stati Uniti.

VI° Il Signor Cav: Uff: Enrico Caruso si obbliga di cantare non più di tre volte alla settimana e non meno di due ma non mai due rappresentazioni di seguito, riservandosi però il diritto di cantare anche un numero maggiore di recite per settimana per compensare quelle che avesse potuto perdere per malattia

VII° Ciascuna rappresentazione in più delle venticinque assicurate verrà pagata al Signor Cav: Uff: Enrico Caruso in ragione di Fr. Cinquemila (fr 5.000)

VIII° Il Signor Cav: Ufficiale Enrico Caruso non sarà obbligato che ad una sola prova di pianoforte ed a una di orchestra

IX° Per i concerti nei quali il Signor Cav: Uff: Enrico Caruso dovesse prender parte e non fossero dati per conto del

il Signor Cav: Uff: Enrico Caruso dipenderà da questo e la paga, da stabilirsi di comune accordo, sarà divisa in modo che i due terzi spettino all'artista e un terzo alla Società dedotte prima tutte le spese che la Società avrà incontrate per la circostanza.

X° Il repertorio del Signor Cav: Ufficiale Enrico Caruso è il seguente:

"Mr. Chevalier Officer Enrico Caruso the trips paid for three persons in I class and two in II class from Europe to America and back and also the trips and luggage necessary for the stay in the United States.

VI- Mr. Chevalier Officer Enrico Caruso

Is obliged to accept not more than three times a week and not less than two but never two performances one after the other, however, reserving the right to sing also a greater number of performances a week to compensate those that he may have lost due to illness.

VII - Each performance in excess of the assured twenty five will be paid to Mr. Chevalier Officer Enrico Caruso at the rate of Fr. Five thousand (Fr. 5,000)

VIII - Mr. Chevalier Officer Enrico Caruso will be obliged only to one rehearsal with piano and one with orchestra.

IX - For the concerts in which Mr. Chevalier Officer Enrico Caruso should take part and were not given by .... Mr. Chevalier Officer Enrico Caruso will depend from this one and the pay, to be established in common agreement, will be divided so that two thirds will go to the artist and one third to the society having deducted all expenses, which the Society may have incurred in the circumstance.

X - The repertoire of Mr. Chevalier Officer Enrico Caruso is the following:"

Mefistofele - Aida - Rigoletto - Traviata - Ballo in Ma=
schera - Regina di Saba - Lucia - Cavalleria - Elixir d'Amore
Favorita - Gioconda - Tosca - Pagliacci - Boheme -
Don Giovanni - Manon Puccini - Lucrezia Borgia -
Fedora - Adriana Lecouvreur - Iris - Carmen - Faust
Pescatori di Perle - Navarrese.
XI° L'opera di debutto verrà scelta di comune accordo
XII° La Società
avrà il diritto di rescindere il presente contrat=
to in caso d'incendio, guerra, lutto nazionale
intimazione governativa o qualunque altro
caso di forza maggiore
XIII° Il presente contratto avrà forza e valore di at=
to pubblico come fatto innanzi a notaio o
vistato dai Consoli e dopo la firma non
potrà essere reciso se non nei casi previsti
di cui all'Art. Dodici (Art XII). Mancando
una delle parti all'adempimento degli ob=
blighi del presente contratto pagherà a tito=
lo di penale la somma di Franchi Ses=
santamila (fr. 60.000)
XIV° Se al giorno otto Aprile il Signor Cav. Ufficiale
Enrico Caruso non saprà che i depositato
presso la Banca Commerciale in Milano
franchi venticinquemila (fr 25.000) della
garanzia e anticipo il presente contratto
si ritiene annullato.

"Mefistofele - Aida - Rigoletto - Traviata - Ballo in Maschera - Regina di Saba - Lucia - Cavalleria - Elixir d'Amore - Favorita - Gioconda - Tosca - Pagliacci - Bohéme - Don Giovanni - Manon Puccini - Lucrezia Borgia - Fedora - Adriana Lecouvreur - Iris - Carmen - Faust - Pescatori di Perle - Navorrese.

XI - The debut opera will be chosen by common agreement.

XII - The Society .... Will have the right to rescind this contract in case of fire, war, national mourning, government *injunction or whichever other case owned to a cause beyond control.*

XIII - The present contract will have the strength and value of a public deed as if done before a notary public or witnessed by Consuls and after the signature cannot be rescinded unless in the cases provided for in the Art. Twelve (Art. XII). One of the parties missing to comply to the obligations of this contract will pay as penalty the sum of Francs Sixty thousand (Fr. 60,000).

XIV - If on April eight Mr. Chevalier Officer Enrico Caruso will not be notified that Francs twenty five thousand (Fr. 25,000) for the guarantee and down payment were deposited at the Banca Commerciale in Milano the present contract will be null."

Amendments

The Vaults of the Safe Deposit Companies in the Equitable Buildings in New York, Boston and St. Louis are the most secure in the World.

STRONGEST IN THE WORLD.

THE EQUITABLE LIFE ASSURANCE SOCIETY

OF THE UNITED STATES.

HENRY B. HYDE, FOUNDER.

I. S. LAWRENCE, GENERAL AGENT.
OFFICE: 120 BROADWAY ROOM 707, (ENTRANCE 81 CEDAR ST.), N. Y.
TELEPHONE: 5800 CORTLANDT.

NEW YORK.

Art. 9th

Per i concerti nei quali il Sig.r Enrico Caruso dovrà prender parte, sian questi dati per conto della Società o d'altri, il Sig.r Caruso dipenderà sempre dalla ~~Compa~~ Società ~~gnia~~ stessa ricevendo per ogni concerto la paga come per una recita e cioè di 6000 franchi se per la stagione 1904-5; di 7000 franchi se per la stagione 1905-6; di 7500 franchi se per le stagioni 1906-7 and 1907-8.

"Art. 9th - For the concerts in which Mr. Enrico Caruso will have to take part, be it on behalf of the Society or others, Mr. Caruso will depend from the same Society receiving for every concert payment as if for one performance and that is

6,000 francs if for the season 1904-5; 7,000 francs if for the season 1905-6; and 7,500[52] francs if for the seasons 1906-7 and 1907-8.

P[asquale]"

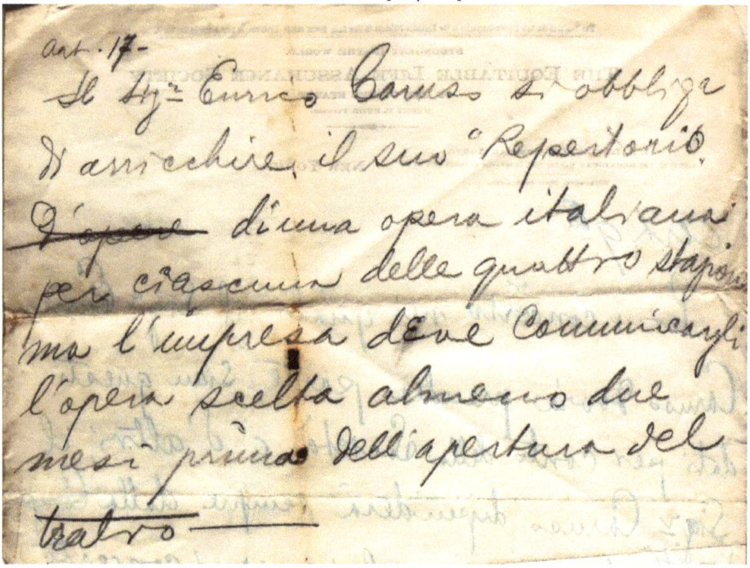

Art. 17-
Il Sig.r Enrico Caruso si obbliga
d'arricchire il suo "Repertorio"
~~d'opere~~ di una opera italiana
per ciascuna delle quattro stagioni
ma l'impresa deve comunicargli
l'opera scelta almeno due
mesi prima dell'apertura del
teatro

"Art. 17 - Mr. Enrico Caruso is obliged to enrich his 'Repertoire' of an Italian Opera for each of the four seasons but the society must communicate to him the chosen opera at least two months before the opening of the theatre."

---

[52] Refer to Giovanni's postcard dated 4/3/1901 number 31 (he was alerting Caruso to request payments in scudi, see note 28). In 1904, $1 US gold = ₤5.18 Italian Liras and = ₣5.18 French Francs (*Cf.* Hering, *Ready reference tables...*, p. 165). In 2012, 1oz$_{(=28.34gr)}$ of gold= \$1,699$_{(=\ \$59.95)}$; \$1 US gold$_{(=1.672gr)}$ = \$100.23. Therefore, considering present inflation and gold values, Caruso was receiving in today's prices the equivalent of \$116,096$_{(x\ 6,000=\ \$1,158)}$, \$135,445$_{(xF\ 7,000=\ \$1,351)}$ and \$145,120$_{(xF\ 7,500=\ \$1,447)}$ for each recital.

With the new Metropolitan engagement, the first use Caruso could think of for his fortune was to send some money to his family. Therefore, on December 16, 1903 Enrico sent to his father Marcellino in Naples the sum of £400 Lire.[53]

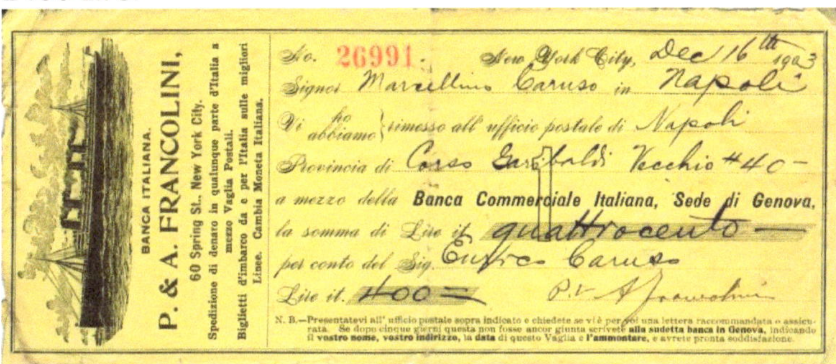

BANCA ITALIANA.
P. & A. FRANCOLINI,
60 Spring St., New York City.
Spedizione di denaro in qualunque parte d'Italia a mezzo Vaglia Postali.
Biglietti d'imbarco da e per l'Italia sulle migliori Linee. Cambia Moneta Italiana.

No. 26991. New York City, Dec 16th 1903

Signor Marcellino Caruso in Napoli

Vi ho/abbiamo rimesso all' ufficio postale di Napoli

Provincia di Corso Garibaldi Vecchio #40 –

a mezzo della Banca Commerciale Italiana, Sede di Genova,

la somma di Lire it. quattrocento —

per conto del Sig. Enrico Caruso

Lire it. 400 =

N. B.—Presentatevi all' ufficio postale sopra indicato e chiedete se vi è per voi una lettera raccommandata o assicurata. Se dopo cinque giorni questa non fosse ancor giunta scrivete **alla sudetta banca in Genova**, indicando il **vostro nome, vostro indirizzo**, la **data** di questo Vaglia e **l'ammontare**, e avrete pronta soddisfazione.

The first year contract between Caruso and the Metropolitan Opera House was renewed for the next four years. Pasquale Simonelli also prepared the new contract. Under Caruso's suggestion, it included his friend, the tenor Mr. Giordani. Therefore, this last one was engaged by the Metropolitan Opera House and sang there during the following season.

From Italy, Caruso acknowledged receipt of that contact.

[53] About present $8,000.

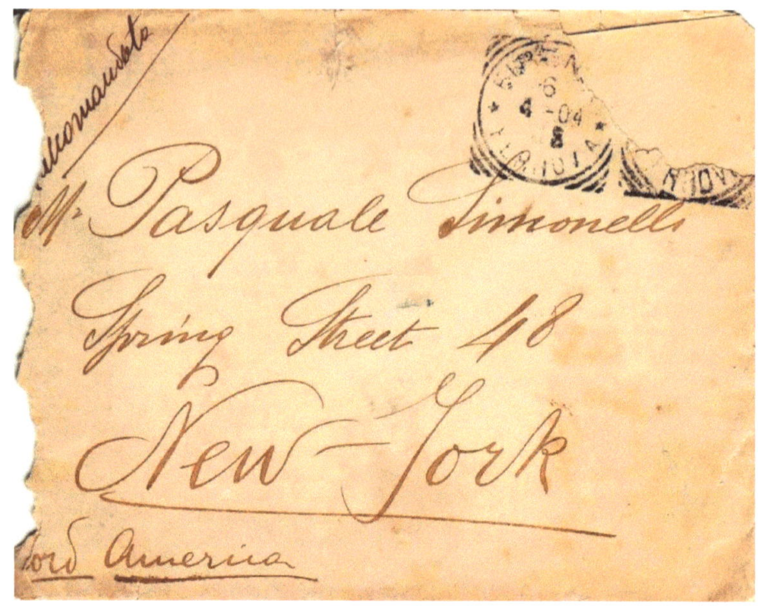

Castello (Presso Firenze) 6/4/904

Carissimo D. Pasqualino.

In possesso vostra gradita del 20 Marzo e telegramma del 28 stesso mese, solo oggi mi è potuto dare rispondere.
Vi ringrazio anche a nome del Sig. Giordani per il contratto e sono sicuro che il Sig. Conrich non troverò quello che gli avevo detto. Non appena sarò a Parigi ove trovasi il Giordani farò firmare il contratto e ve ne farò regolare spedizione.

....

"Castello (near Florence) April 4th, 1904. Very dear Don Pasqualino. I received your appreciated letter of March 20th and the telegram of the 28th of the same month, only today I was able to answer.

I thank you for the contract also in behalf of Mr. Giordani and I am sure that Mr. Conried will not find that which I had told him. As soon as I will be in Paris, where Giordani is, I will have him sign the contract and I will duly mail it to you.."

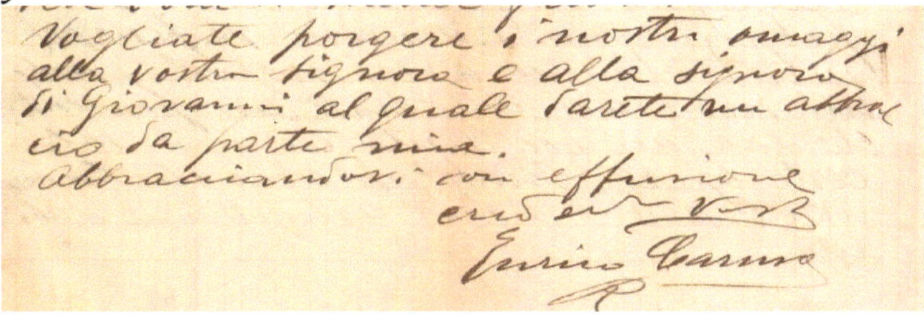
Vogliate porgere i nostri omaggi alla vostra signora e alla signora di Giovanni al quale farete un abbraccio da parte mia.
Abbracciandovi con effusione
[illegible] vostro
Enrico Caruso

"... Please give our regards to your wife and to Giovanni's wife. Give him an embrace for me. Embracing you with effusion and reverence, yours Enrico Caruso."

As time went by, an unfortunate misunderstanding stubbornly convinced Caruso not to continue Pasquale as his agent. Only later, when certain facts unknown to the tenor were cleared, Caruso returned to Pasquale admitting that he had been wrong.[54]

However, the friendship between the two men remained intact for all the years to come.

[54] *Cf.* Key, *Enrico Caruso*, P. 172.

CHAPTER 3
Postcards from Pasquale in Caruso's personal collection

"Nov. 20, 1903. My dear Don Pasqualino,[55] *going back home last evening I found your postcard. Thanks, thanks, thanks. Wife feeling better, and as soon as she can, that is go out, it will be our care to exchange the visit to your sister in law and at the same time stuff myself with beans. Affectionate regards your ECaruso."*

Like his brother Giovanni, Pasquale I. Simonelli started mailing a numbered series of postcards to Caruso.

---

[55] Pasquale, with a term of endearment.

April 12, 1904 from New York to Caruso in his Florentine Villa Le Panche

"NY 4/12. P.I.Simonelli."

Postkarte — Carte postale
Weltpostverein — Union postale universelle
Levelező-Lap — Correspondenzkarte —
Dopisnice — Karta korespondencyjna —
Korespondenční lístek — Briefkaart —
Cartolina postale — Post card — Brefkort
Открытое-письмо - Дописна Карта
Tarjeta postal

M. P. Simonelli
Spring Street 48
New York
Nord America

Gruss aus Prag. - Panorama von Hradschin.

5/5/904 Caro D. Pasqualino
In possesso di 13 vostre cartoline vi ringrazio immensamente, epperò aspetto vostra lettera promessami onde avere il piacere di leggervi.

Prague, Czechoslovakia

I "5/5/904. *Dear Don Pasqualino. I received 13 of your postcards and I thank you immensely, however, I am waiting for your letter you promised me, so to have the pleasure of reading you. Caruso.*"

Missing cards number II, III, IV

Dopisnice — Postkarte — Levelező-Lap
Karta korespondencyjna CARTE POSTALE Cartolina postale
Union postale universelle Weltpostverein Unione postale universale
Открытое Письмо

M. P. Simonelli
Spring St. 48
New York
Nord America

V
teatro un tale successo e i tedeschi tanto entusiasti: bissai tutti i pezzi e bissai la canzone dell'ultimo atto. Dopo qui il 14.

PRAG
Hybernergasse mit Staatsbahnhof.

"V ... theatre such a success and the Germans very enthused. I gave encores on all pieces and

repeated the three times the song of the last act.[56]
After the 14th..."

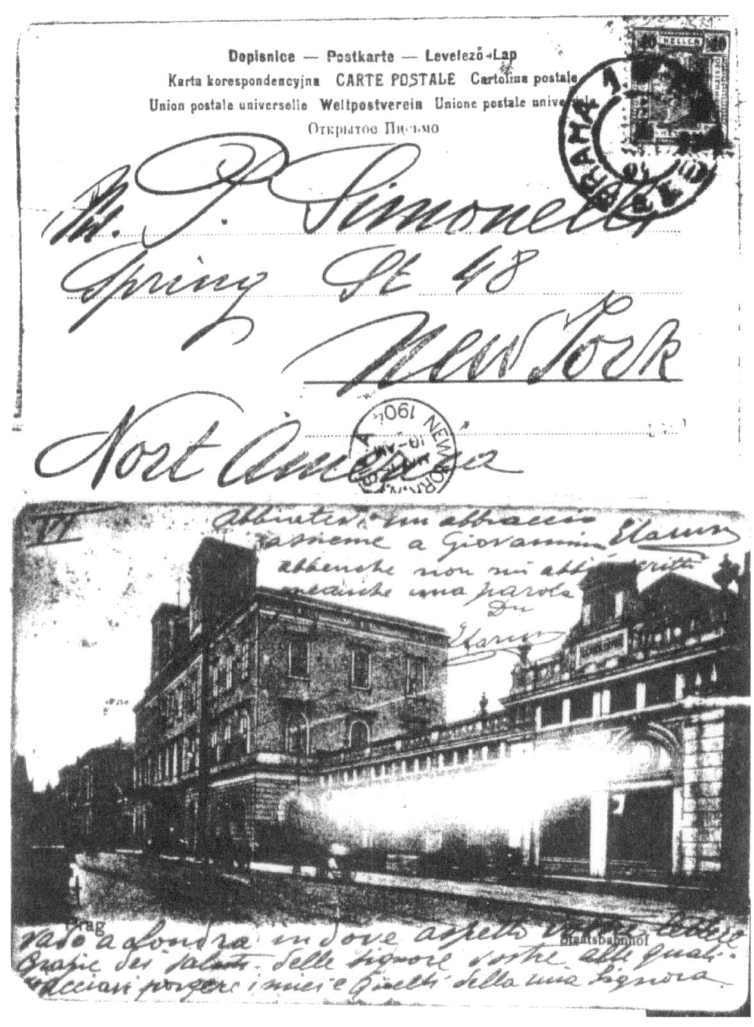

---

[56] We do not know of which opera. However, it could have been on in the role of Assad (in Goldmark's *The Queen of Sheba*) or of Lohengrin (Wagner's *Lohengrin*).

"VI... I will go to London where I will be expecting your letters. Thank you for the greetings of your ladies to whom please extend mine and those of my wife. Receive an embrace together with Giovanni, even if he did not write to me, not even a word. Don ECaruso."

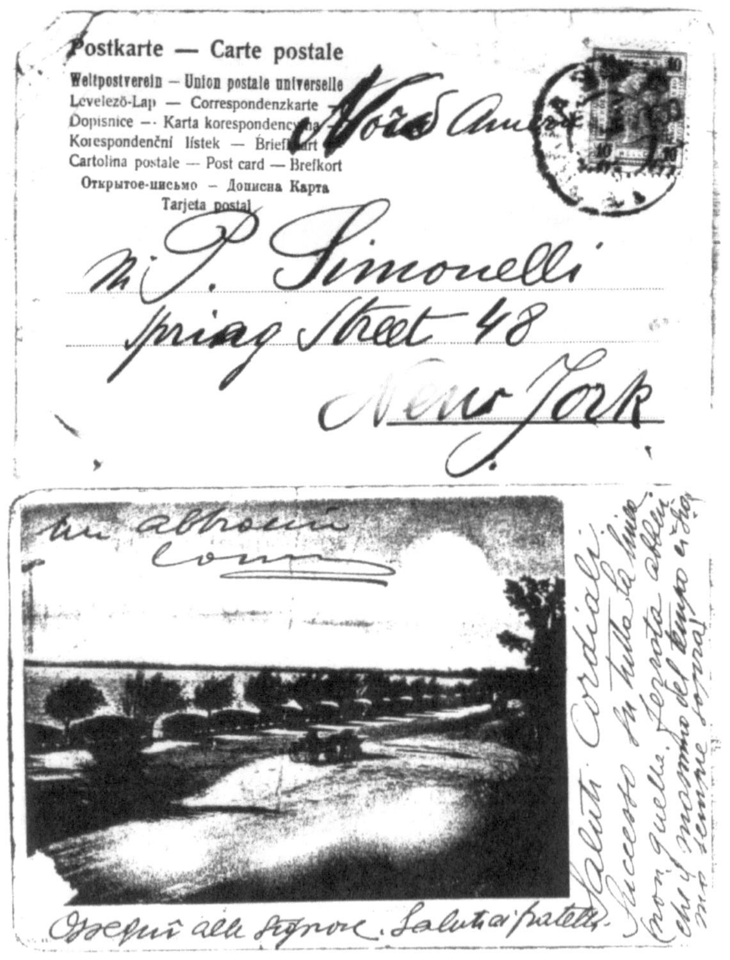

Postkarte — Carte postale

Weltpostverein — Union postale universelle

Levelező-Lap — Correspondenzkarte

Dopisnice — Karta korespondency[jna]

Korespondenční lístek — Brief[kaart]

Cartolina postale — Post card — Brefkort

Открытое-письмо — Дописна Карта

Tarjeta postal

Nord America

P. Simonelli

Spring Street 48

New York

Ossequi alle Signore. Saluti ai fratelli.

Germany, May 1904

"Cordial greetings. Success all along the line (not the railroad line even if most of the time we are always on it). Regards to the ladies. Greetings to the brothers."

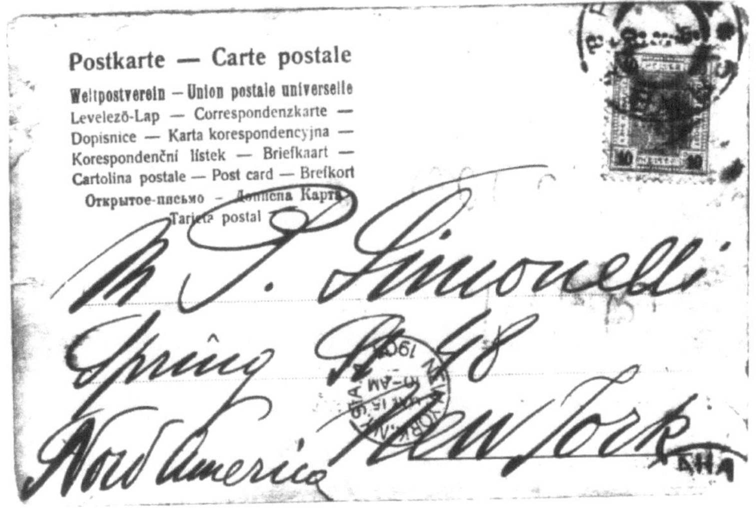

Hamburg, Germany May 15th, 1904,
aboard a boat of the *Große Hafenrundfahrt*, *Fleetfahrt*

(harbor and canal boat tour)

"Before leaving this boat (tomorrow) I send regards. Caruso."

On May 15, 1904, Pasquale mailed a series of postcards [1 t0 18] to Caruso who was staying at the Covent Garden Theatre in London.

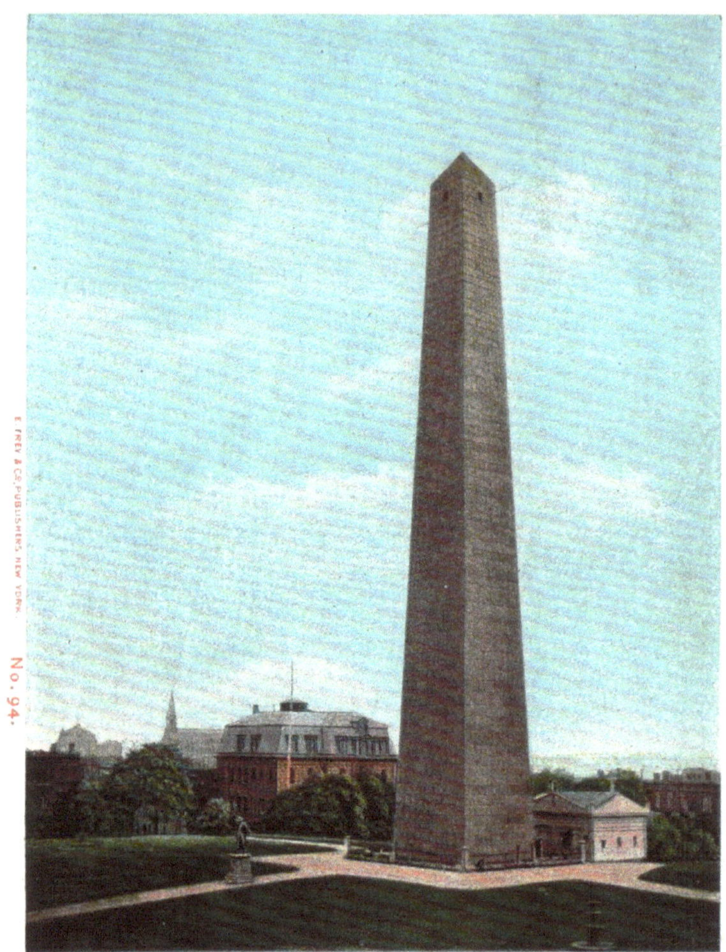

BUNKER HILL MONUMENT, CHARLESTOWN, Mass.

N.Y. 15 luglio 1904.

Illustrissimo Sig.r Caruso,

Ieri giunse a questo
R.o Consolato la nomina

"NY July 15, 1904 Very Illustrious Mr. Caruso, Yesterday arrived at this Royal Consulate the nomination..."

"2 ... of our Mr. Conried to Cavalier of the Italian Crown. I did not miss to telegraph you in Berlin because..."

Post Card

Illmo.
Comm. Enrico Caruso
Covent Garden Theatre
London
England

THIS SIDE FOR THE ADDRESS.

VIRGINIA ARLINGTON MEMORIAL GARDEN, WASHINGTON. D. C.

3 alcuni giorni prima Egli
m'aveva telegrafato da
quella città per sapere
Contemporaneamente
al Sig. Conried telegrafai

" *3* ... some days earlier you had telegraphed me from that city to be informed. Concomitantly I telegraphed Mr. Conried..."

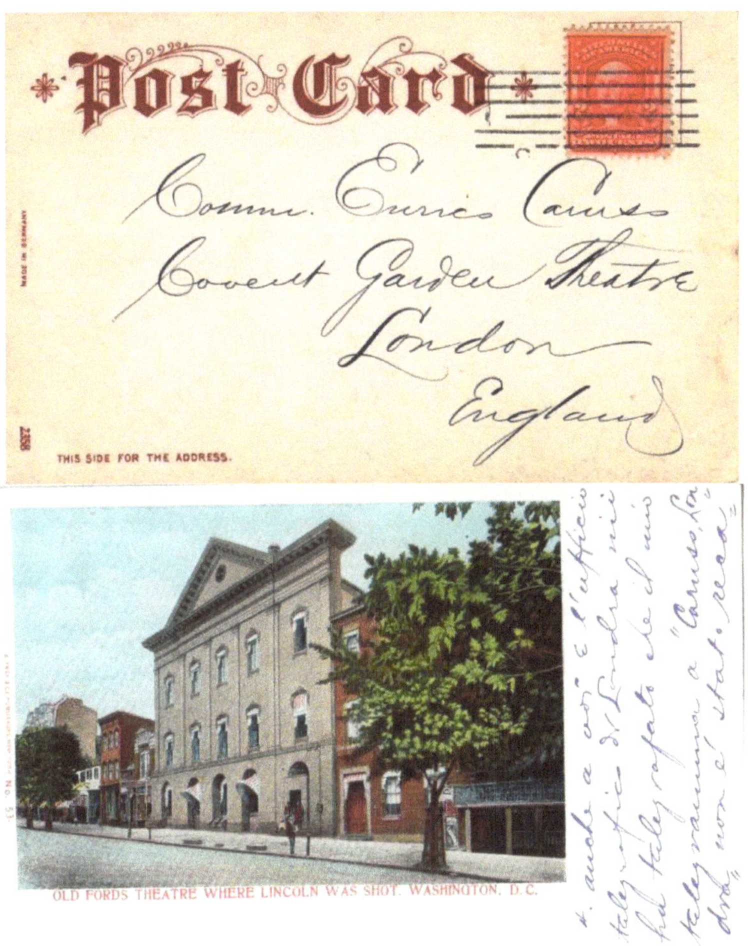

"4 ... and you. But London's telegraphic office telegraphed me that my telegraph to 'Caruso London" was not deli[vered]..."

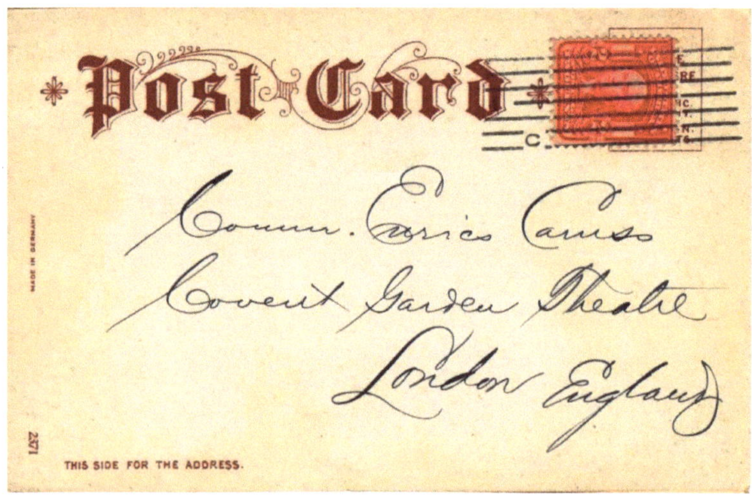

How it is possible" Caruso is known in the entire world.
Who does not know him?

5/ pitato perché "unKnown," Pizzi & f... orboni, non si recapita un telegram ma a "Caruso in Londra"

"5 ... [deli]*vered because 'unknown.' Pieces of smart...s, a telegram to 'Caruso in London' is not delivered...*"

[is it possible?]

Cards n. 6 - 7 are missing

BRIDGE OVER WALK CENTRAL PARK, WINTER SCENE, NEW YORK.

"8 ... *congratulations to the Impresario who cares especially for yours, which are those of his beloved Caruso...*"

Which are the things the Impresario cares for? We do not know.
Cards n. 9 - 10 are missing

"11- ... anche un'affettuosa mammina - Ed è a quell'affetto che io debbo la buona fortuna d'aver mangiato dei cimmoli squisitamente indimenticabili - Perchè mi trascura le omettendo di mandarmi anche qualche giornale

"11- ... also a very affectionate mommy - And it is to that affection that I owe the good fortune of having eaten exquisitely unforgettable morsels -

Why you neglect me omitting to send me also some newspaper…"

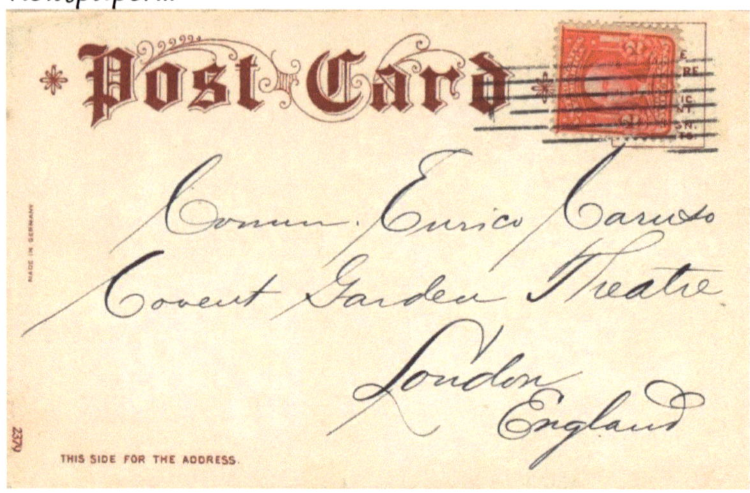

"12…[newspaper] *from London, which write about your successes and about your triumphs? I passed the one you sent me from Prague to Kobbé,*[57] *critic of the NY Herald, who wrote a nice article about you, and I will send it to you as soon as Paris will*

[57] Gustav Kobbé, (1857 - 1918) author of *The Complete Opera Book*.

have translated it in his Review since the translation written in the [evening] *Bulletin..*"

13. della sera non mi va e l'ho cestinato.
Le sole monete commemorative per l'Esposizione
di St Louis sono dei dollari d'oro - sono di
tre categorie e l'amico mio di St. Louis mi
scrive che costano tre dollari l'una ma

"13 ... the evening [*Bulletin*] *I do not like and I threw it in the waste-paper basket - The only commemorative coins for the St Louis Exposition*[58]

---

[58] The 100th year of the Louisiana Purchase Exposition: The 1904 St. Louis World's Fair. Caruso was also a stamp and coin

are gold dollars - They are of three categories and my friend from St Louis writes to me that they cost three dollars each whi[le]…"

1903-4 THREE TYPES
$ 1 COMMEMORATIVE GOLD COINS FOR THE
100TH YEAR OF THE LOUISIANA PURCHASE EXPOSITION:

1) ob. JEFFERSON 2) ob. MCKINLEY[59]

3) ob. CLARK – re. LEWIS

collector.

[59] 1 and 2 have the same re.[verse].

Post Card

Comm. Enric Caruso
Covent Garden Theatre
London
England

THIS SIDE FOR THE ADDRESS.

WHITE HOUSE, NORTH FRONT, WASHINGTON, D.C.

14. te di valore reale non v'è che un dollaro -
Io penserei di procurarvene uno di ciascuna
categoria - Ne vorreste forse di più?
aspetto i vostri desideri al riguardo
Quando scrivete in Italia

"14... [whi]le in real value it is not worth more than a dollar - I would think of acquiring one of each category for you - Would you like more? I am waiting for your wishes in the matter. When you write to Italy..."

Post Card

PLACE

Enrico Caruso Esq.
Covent Garden Theatre
London
England

MADE IN GERMANY

2307 THIS SIDE FOR THE ADDRESS.

STATE, WAR and NAVY BUILDING, WASHINGTON. D. C.

15
fatemi la cortesia di ricordarci alla signora
a cui facciamo pure sentiti auguri pel prossimo
lieto evento – La mia signora, Giulia e tutti
i miei fratelli, grati d'essersi ricordati

"15 … do me the courtesy to remind us to your wife to whom we express our felt wishes for the next happy event[60] – My wife, Giulia and all my brothers, are grateful to you for having remembered…"

---

[60] Enrico Caruso Jr. was to be born that same year.

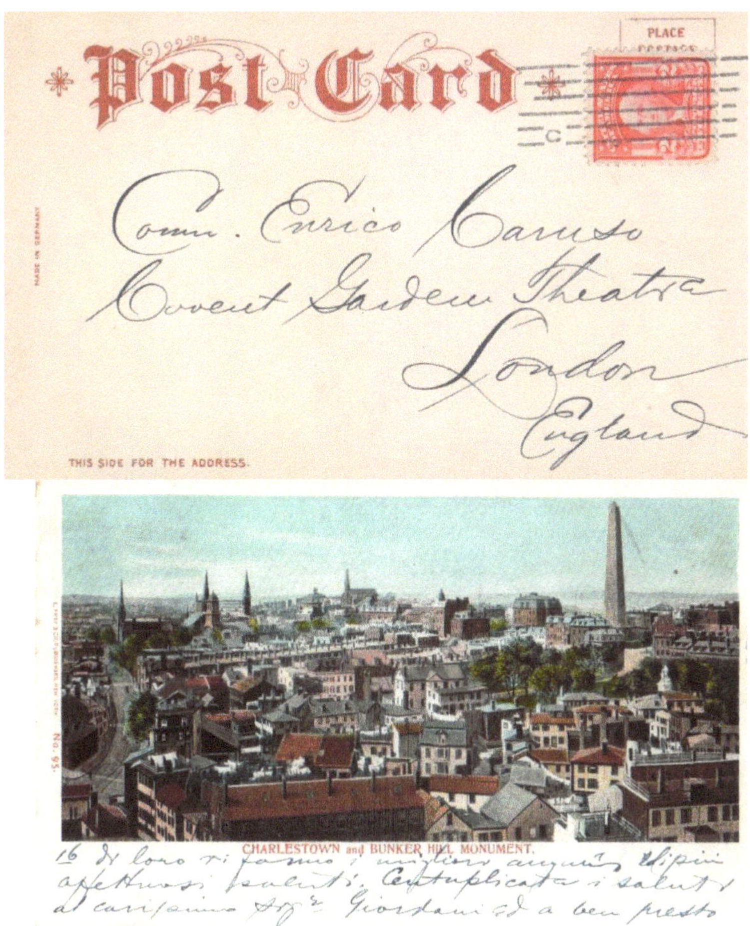

"16... them express their best wishes and the most heartfelt greetings. Hundredfold greetings to the very dear Mr. Giordani[61] *and till the next time..."*

[61] Tenor Giordani sung in 1904 at the Met. under Conried, in *Aida* (11/ 21), *Lucia di Lammermoor* (11/24), *La Traviata* (11/26).

"17... seeing you - Where will I send my postcards after London? Be so courteous to let me know - with a very affectionate embrace..."

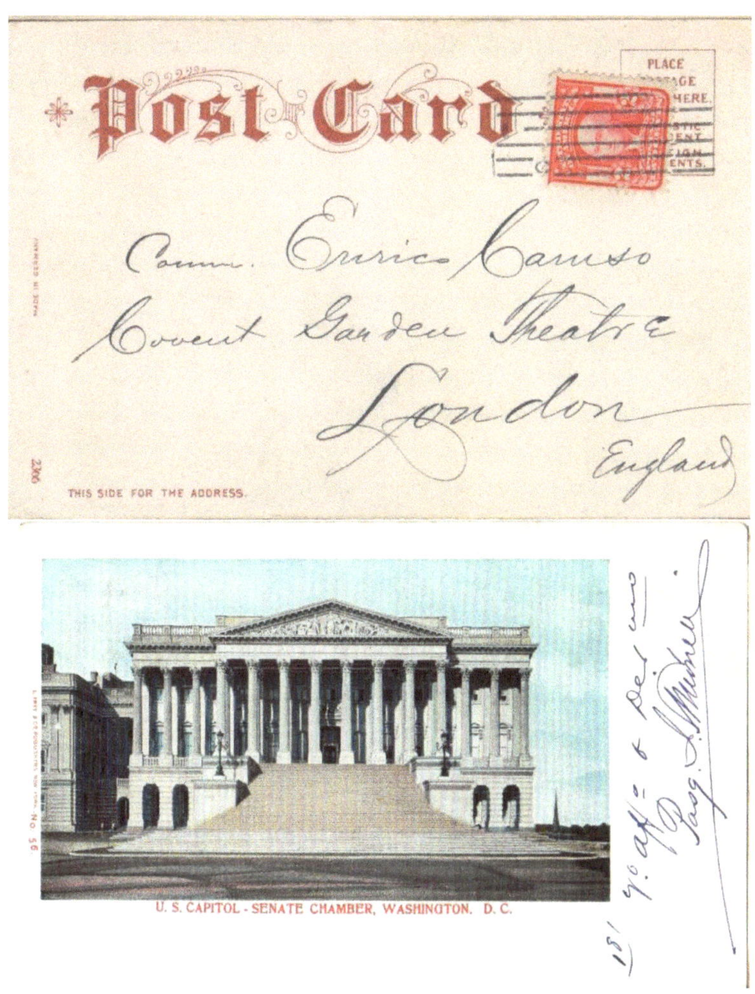

"18 ... your very affectionate and very devout Pasquale I, Simonelli."

Post Card

Comm. Enrico Caruso
Covent Garden Theatre
London
England

THIS SIDE FOR THE ADDRESS.

Mailed in New York on July 21st, 1904 [1 to 8]

TREASURY BUILDING, WASHINGTON. D. C.

New York 21/7 04.
Buon viaggio e quando in Italia presentate
i miei più sentiti ossequi alla gentilissima
signora Ada - Rammentatemi pure al

"New York, July 21, 04. Have a nice trip and when in Italy offer my most felt regards at your very kind wife Ada[62] *- Remind me also to Conried,*

[62] Ada Giachetti, (Italian soprano previously married to Gino Botti) was

whom you will surely see in Milan or also Florence!......"

Postcards 1 to 7 are missing

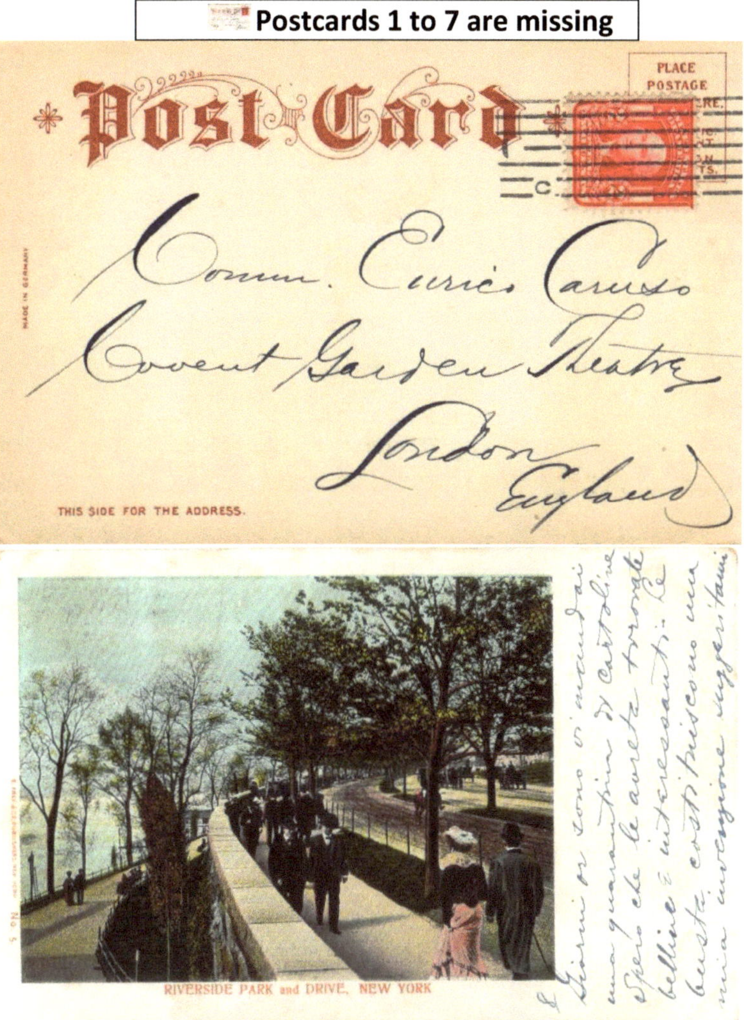

Caruso's partner from 1897 to 1908. This same year Enrico Caruso, Jr. was born and Pasquale Simonelli had his first son Julius.

"8 ... Some days ago I sent you about forty postcards. I hope you found them cute and interesting - The envelopes are my invention suggested by..."

Post card mailed to Pasquale's summer residence,
221 Morris Ave (now Westwood Station), Long Branch, NJ.

"August 4th, 1904. Kind Don Pasqualino. Today Argenti[63] *gave me a postcard you sent me, the postcard of the '<u>big noses</u>,' which enriches my collection of the humoristic cards. I received a newspaper from Paris* [64] *in which I read a lot of stupidities. I will write to him to have him correct certain things that I do not agree. Greetings and regards to your wife and to you a very affectionate embrace, your Caruso."*

---

[63] Caruso's Italian Impresario, "THEATRICAL AGENCY G. ARGENTI & COMP." (Caruso's letter to Pasquale, August 7th, 1902).

[64] See Pasquale's postcard number 12.

Later, on February 7, 1905, from the Hotel York in New York, Caruso specified that Argenti was his only agent for Europe:

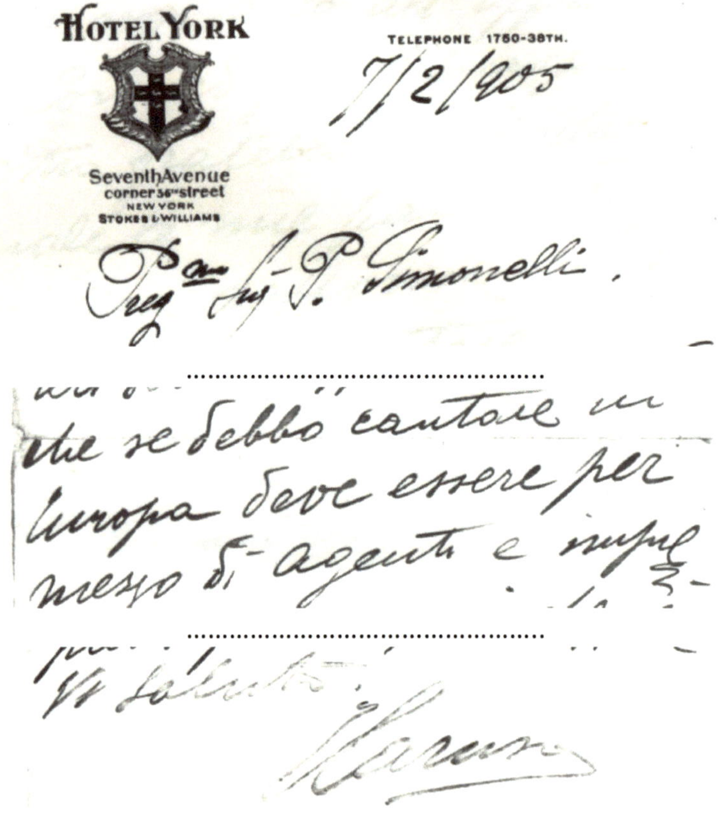

HOTEL YORK

TELEPHONE 1750-38TH.

7/2/1905

Seventh Avenue
corner 36th street
NEW YORK
STOKES & WILLIAMS

Preg.mo Sig. P. Simonelli.

....

che se debbo cantare in
Europa deve essere per
mezzo di agenti e sempre

....

Vi saluto.

Caruso

"2/7/905. Esteemed Mr. P. Simonelli ... if I must sing in Europe it must be through Argenti... greeting ECaruso."

CARTOLINA POSTALE
(CARTE POSTALE
NEW YOR
NOV 20
11 AM
Pasquale Simonelli
Spring Street 48
City

November 20th, 1904 on Italian postcard mailed in NY, Caruso wrote,.

"Dear Don Pasqualino, Last night Pagliacci and, in spite of a swollen face, I had my name

engraved in the theatre - Give my best to your wife. Caruso."

Mailed in New York April 1, 1905

"IV ... finally I spent some days home and then I came in this country to sing only 3 performances. I made my performance last night and it was never seen in this..."

Cards V missing

POST CARD

THE ADDRESS TO BE WRITTEN ON THIS SIDE

Hand delivered?

CARUSO.

10/3/905

Caro [illegible] Pasqualino

Grazie per le 10 cartoline molto interessanti per me.

Dopo Lucia e Pagliacci passerà Gioconda e spero avere lo stesso successo malgrado i [illegible]

Spero che non sia nulla perchè se seguita può portare cattive cose

[illegible]

"Boston [?] March 10th, 1905. Dear Don Pasqualino, Thank you for the 10 postcards very interesting for me. After *Lucia*[65] and *Pagliacci*

[65] *Lucia di Lammermoor* by Donizetti.

tonight Gioconda[66] and I hope I will have the same success in spite of the mumps, I hope it is nothing because if it keeps on can lead to bad consequences for anyone. My wife is here only to make sure I take better care of myself. Tomorrow we leave for Pittsburg. My regards to all in the family. Caruso"

From Chicago, Caruso writes,

Congress Hotel Co.
R. H. SOUTHGATE PRESIDENT
OPERATING THE AUDITORIUM THE ANNEX APARTMENT BUILDING.
Chicago 23/3 1905
Preg. D. Pasqualino.

....

apparire. Sono contento perche le cose vanno bene e la fatica non mi ha fatto nulla ne sulla voce e ne sulla salute. I mumps sono spariti e tutti dicono che mi hanno fatto venire la voce più bella.

"Chicago March 23, 1905. Very Esteemed Don Pasqualino... I am happy because things are going well and hard work did affect neither my voice

---

[66] By Ponchielli.

nor my heath. The <u>mumps</u> are gone and everyone says that they made my voice more beautiful..."

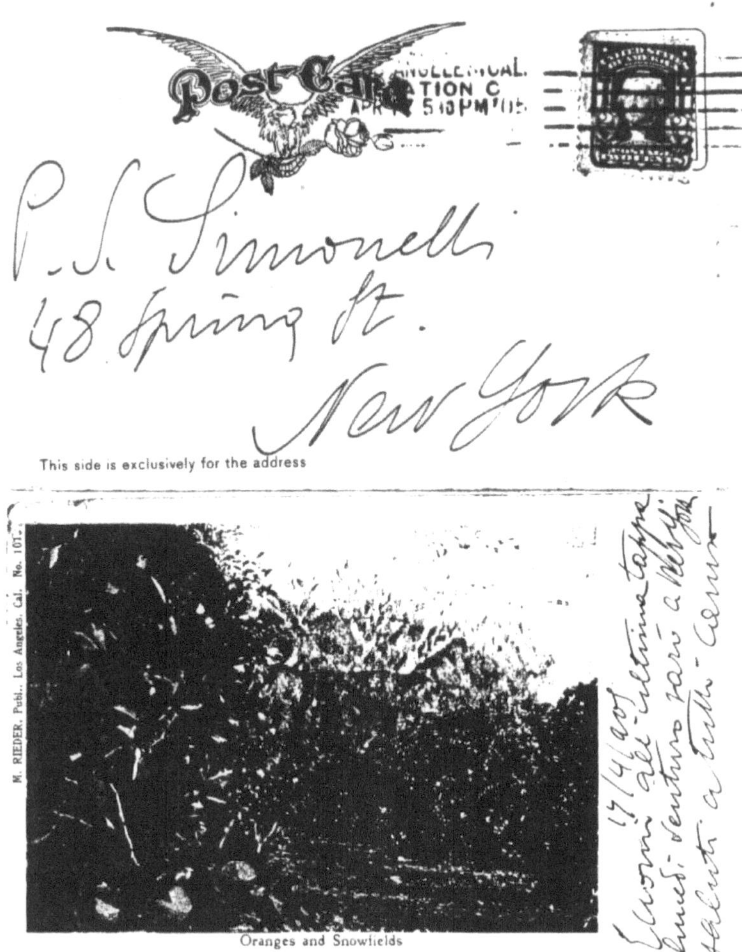

"April 17th, 905. Here I am at the last leg of the journey. Next Monday I will be in New York. Regards to all - Caruso."

End of postcards

CHAPTER 4
Further correspondences with Caruso

The friendly correspondence between Enrico and Pasquale continued uninterrupted. From Villa Le Panche, in Castello, near Florence, Caruso writes,

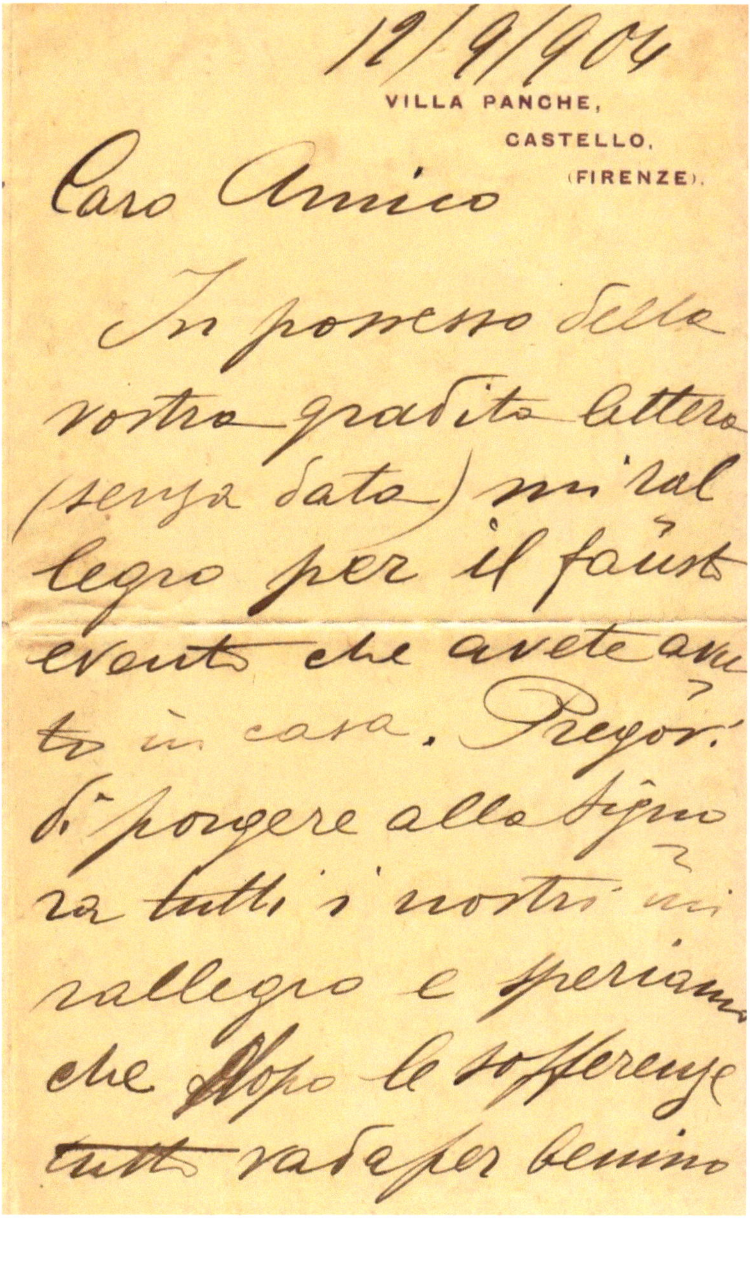

12/9/904

VILLA PANCHE,
CASTELLO,
(FIRENZE).

Caro Amico

In possesso della vostra gradita lettera (senza data) mi ral-legro per il fausto evento che avete avu-to in casa. Pregovi di porgere alla Signo-ra tutti i nostri mi rallegro e speriamo che ~~dopo~~ le sofferenze ~~tutto~~ vada per benino

"Dear friend, I received your appreciated letter (without date) I am happy for the blissful event[67] you had home. Please give your wife all our wishes. I am pleased and let us hope that after the suffering all is good..."

[67] Pasquale's son Julius was born on July 25, 1904 in Long Branch N.J. (died on February 8, 1946 in San Paolo Belsito, prov. Of Naples, Italy)

Come vi telegrafai
anche la mia signora
la mattina del 7 c. alle
ore 7 ant. diede alla
luce un bel bambino.
Non sto qui a farvi
la descrizione della
cosa perchè già sape
te però, vi debbo dire
che il secondo figlio
fà provare più emo
zioni del primo perchè
due mesi avanti io
non potevo avvici
nare la signora per

"... As I telegraphed you, also my wife the morning of the 7th current month at 7 am brought to life a beautiful baby boy.[68] Here, I am not describing the event because you already know. However, I must tell you that the second son makes you feel more emotions than the first one[69] because two months prior I could not get close to my wife for..."

paura di farle male e al
momento dello sgravo mi
son messo con la testa fra
le coltri e ò pianto per cin
que ore continuatamente
tanto vero che, chi mi vede
va mi domandava se ero io quel
lo che aveva sgravato perchè
avevo la faccia cadaverica
mentre la Signora era bella
e fresca.
Grazie a Dio essa e il bim
bo godono buona salute
Al bimbo è stato dato il nome
di Enrico per due ragioni
per il padre e per Enrico.

....

[68] Enrico Jr. (Mimmi) September 7, 1904, died April 9, 1987.
[69] Rodolfo (Fofò) born on July 2, 1898.

"... I was afraid I could hurt her and, at the moment of conception I put my head between the blankets and I cried continuously for five hours, so much so that who saw me after asked me if it was I that had labored because I had a cadaveric face while my wife was beautiful and fresh.
Thank God she and the baby are in good health. To the baby was given the name Enrico on account of the father and for Conried ..."

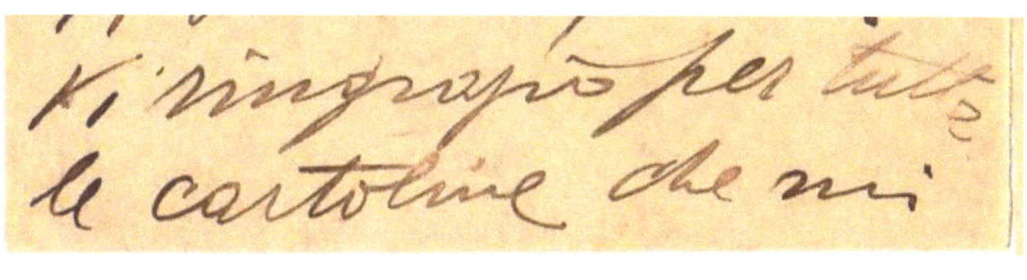
Ti ringrazio per tutte
le cartoline che mi

....

"... Thank you for all the postcards, which I ..."

sono tutte arrivate
Non posso essere costì
in ottobre perche ho qui
ancora molte cose
a fare
Grazie degli articoli
e francobolli.
Volete farmi il piace
re di ringraziarmi
il Sig Del Pappa e Pu
gione? Grazie!
Pregovi ossequiare
la vostra signora
dalla nostra parte
e augurarle ~~tutt~~ il
bene possibile e imma
ginabile
Abbracciandovi
vostro
Caruso

"... received all. I cannot be there [in New York] in October because I have still many things to do here.
Thank you for the newspaper articles and the stamps. Can you please thank for me Mr. Del Papa[70] *e Frugone?*[71] *Yes thanks? Please give our regards to your wife wishing her all possible and imaginable wellbeing? Embracing you*
Your ECaruso."

70 Dante Del Papa (italian Tenor) (Pisa 1854 - New York 1923).
71 Frank Frugone publisher.

From Minneapolis, Minn., Caruso writes to Pasquale Simonelli,

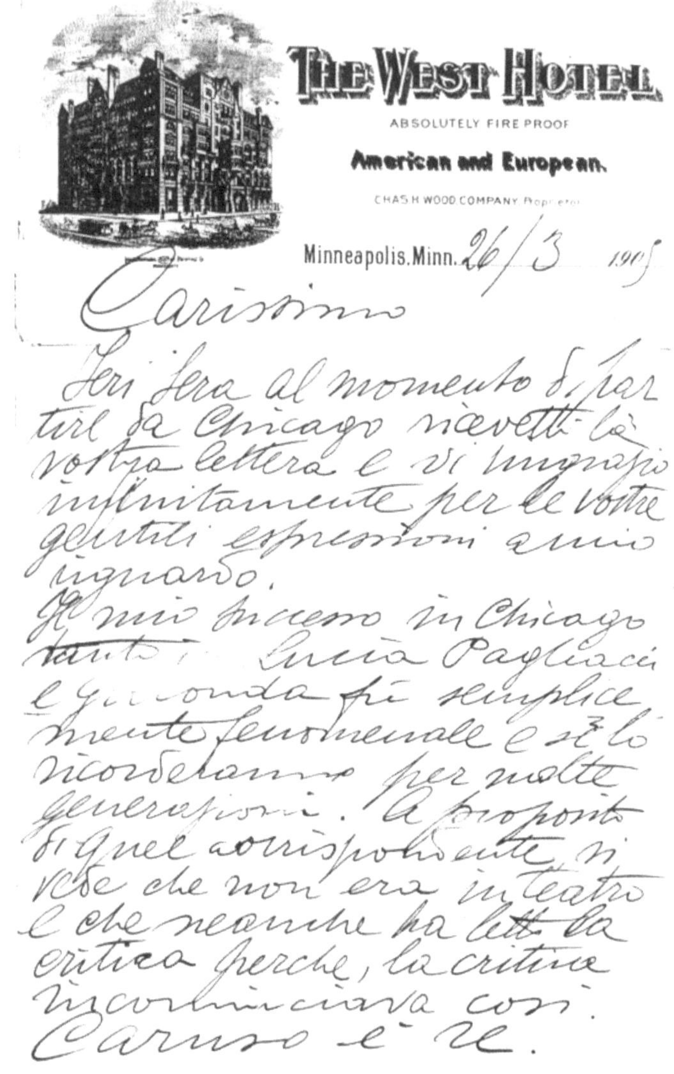

THE WEST HOTEL
ABSOLUTELY FIRE PROOF
American and European.
CHAS. H. WOOD COMPANY, Proprietors

Minneapolis, Minn. 26/3 1905

Carissimo

Ieri sera al momento di partire da Chicago ricevetti la vostra lettera e vi ringrazio infinitamente per le vostre gentili espressioni a mio riguardo.
Il mio successo in Chicago ~~tanto~~ in Lucia Pagliacci e Gioconda fu semplicemente fenomenale e se lo ricorderanno per molte generazioni. A proposito di quel corrispondente si vede che non era in teatro e che neanche ha letto la critica perche, la critica incominciava così: Caruso è re.

"March 26, 1905. Very Dear, Last night at the moment before leaving Chicago I received your letter and I thank you immensely for your kind expression on my behalf.
My success in Chicago, *Lucia, Pagliacci* and *Gioconda* was simply phenomenal and they will remember it for many generations. Regarding that correspondent it seems that he was not in the theatre and that he did not even read the critics, because the critics started with: *Caruso is king*..."

Caruso à rubato tutti
i cuori.
Caruso Wounderfull
e così di seguito. Dunque
si vede che quel signore à
rimasto, nel fare la corris-
pondenza, il mio nome in qualche Coctel. Oppure è qualcu-
no che è venuto da me e
io non lo ho ricevuto perchè sono tante le seccature
che ho che ne ho piene le
tasche.
Scusate che vi scrivo così in fretta
e male perchè sono stanco dal
viaggio.
Per ora nulla di nuovo a
dirvi.
Baciatemi il vostro bimbo
e ossequiatemi la signora
Salutandovi assieme a tutti
i vostri fratelli. Vostro

"... *Caruso has stolen all hearts. Caruso is wonderful and so on. Therefore, it seems that gentlemen, in writing the correspondence, left my name in some folder. Or perhaps he is someone who came to me and I did not receive him because*

I have so many annoyances that I am fed up with it.
Forgive me if I am writing in hurry and bad because I am tired by the trip.
This is all for now. Kiss your child for me and give my regards to the ladies. My best to you together with all your brothers, Believe me ECaruso."

Caruso from London,

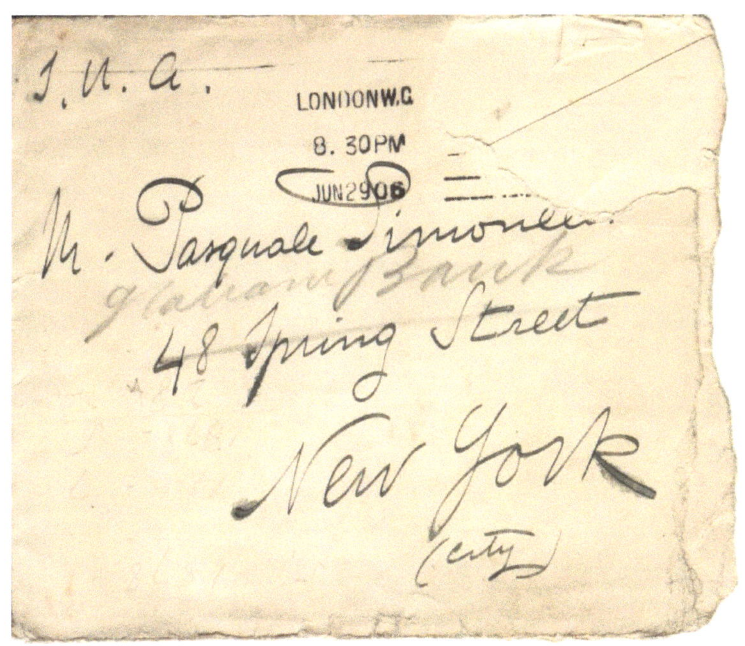

30/6/906
HOTEL CECIL,
LONDON, W.C.

TELEPHONE No. 4662 GERRARD.
TELEGRAMS "CECELIA, LONDON"

Carissimo Pasqualino
Grazie della vostra lettera
e credo sia stato bene il vostro
modo d'agire circa la risposta al Progresso. Molto meglio.
Ho avuto già istruzioni da
Conried circa il repertorio e
in esso vi sono comprese le
opere da voi menzionate.
Per l'altro teatro, nessuno di
da pensiero, perche il pubblico
che va al metropolitan cono-
sce buona porzione degli artisti
che vi sono ingaggiati, e sono

"June 30, 1906. Very dear Pasqualino.
Thank you for your letter and I think that your way of doing regarding the answer to the Progresso[72] was good. Much better. I already received instructions from Conried regarding the repertoire and in it are included the operas mentioned by you. For the other theatre he does

[72] Italian-American Newspaper in New York City.

not give it a thought because the public that goes to the Metropolitan knows a good part of the artists that are engaged in it and I am..."

sicuro che nessuno lascia la
via vecchia per la nuova
In quanto a paragoni vedremo
sulla breccia chi porterà la
palma e chi vi resterà sopra.
La stampa, è stata e sarà
sempre tale; Pagate che dice
bene, non pagate vi ammazza
perciò; quando si fà il proprio
dovere e si hanno i milionari
dalla nostra parte non bisogna
pensarci.
Ho avuto qui il mio solito successo in
Rigoletto, Tosca, Boheme, Pagliacci,
Butterfly e Aida e non si parla che di
me in tutti i circoli e saloni artistici
Caro amico, per avere il successo costante
come ho io bisogna essere assolutamen
te, vegetariano...!!!
Mille saluti alle famiglie e a voi una stretta di mano
aff. Caruso

"... sure that no one leaves the old road to follow the new one.
Regarding comparisons we shall see in the breach who shall bring the palm and who shall remain in it. The press was and will be always the same. Pay and it speaks well, do not pay it and it will even kill you, when duty is performed and millionaires are on our side we should not think about it.
Here, I had my usual success in *Rigoletto*, *Tosca*, *Bohème*, *Pagliacci*, *Butterfly* and *Aida* and in all artistic circles and salons everybody speaks about me. My dear, to have constant success as I have one must be absolutely vegetarian!!!
A thousand regards to the families and to you a hand shake,
affectionately ECaruso."

Christmas 1915

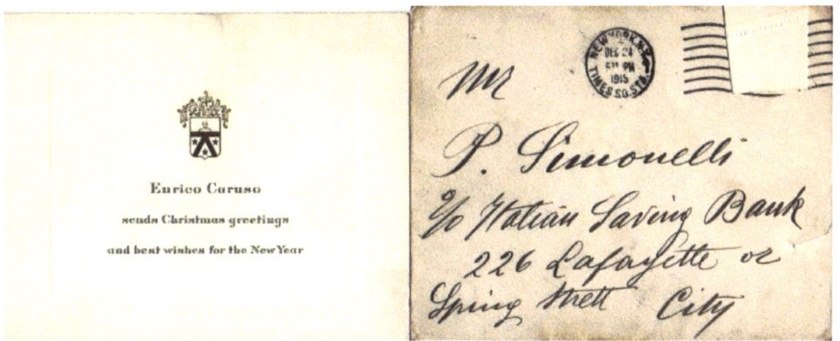

Enrico Caruso

sends Christmas greetings

and best wishes for the New Year

NEW YORK N.Y.
DEC 24
5 PM
1915
TIMES SQ. STA.

Mr
P. Simonelli
c/o Italian Saving Bank
226 Lafayette or
Spring Street City

From New York, Caruso writes,

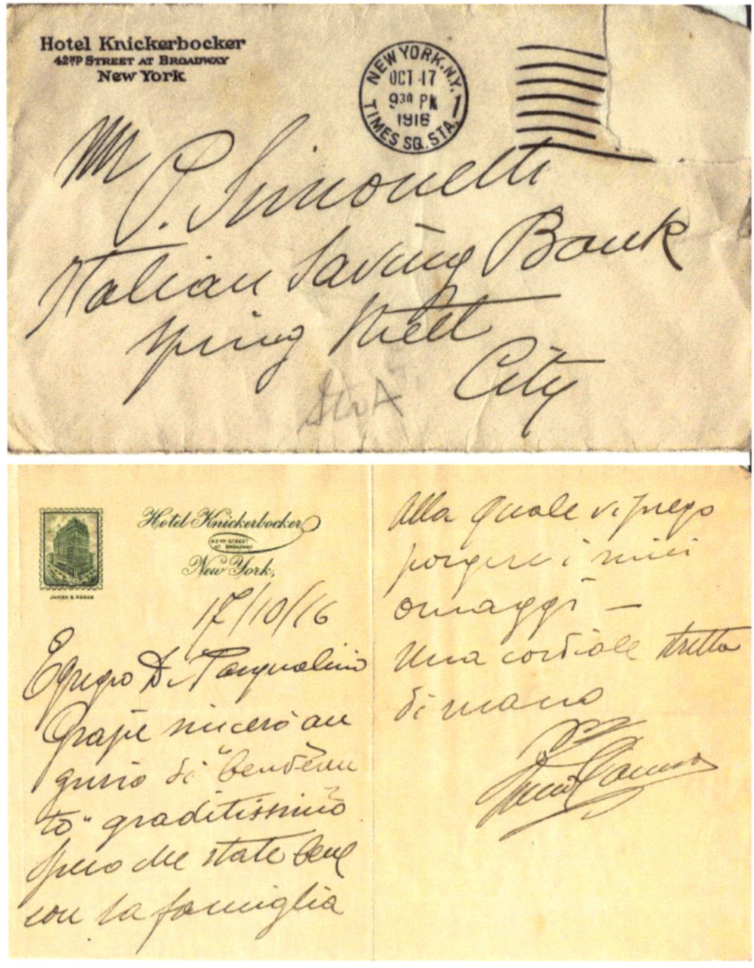

Hotel Knickerbocker
42ND STREET AT BROADWAY
New York

NEW YORK, N.Y. OCT 17 9³⁰ PM 1916 TIMES SQ. STA. 1

Mr P. Simonelli
Italian Saving Bank
Spring Street
City

Hotel Knickerbocker
42ND STREET AT BROADWAY
New York,

17/10/16

Egregio D. Pasqualino
Grazie sincero all'
augurio di "benvenu-
to" graditissimo.
Spero che state bene
con la famiglia
alla quale vi prego
porgere i miei
omaggi –
Una cordiale stretta
di mano
Enrico Caruso

"October 17, 16. Egregious Don Pasqualino, Thank you for your sincere welcome wishes, I appreciated it very much. I hope you are well with the family to *whom please give my respects. A cordial hand shake, yours Enrico Caruso."*

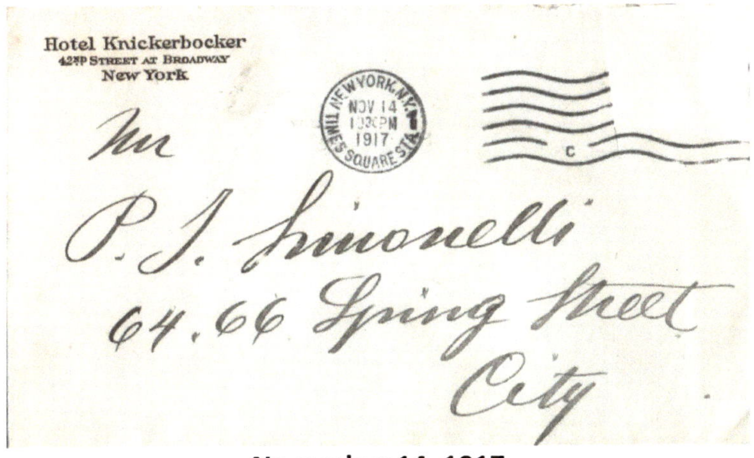

Hotel Knickerbocker
42ND STREET AT BROADWAY
New York

NEW YORK, N.Y.
NOV 14
1917
TIMES SQUARE STA.

Mr
P. J. Simonelli
64.66 Spring Street
City

November 14, 1917

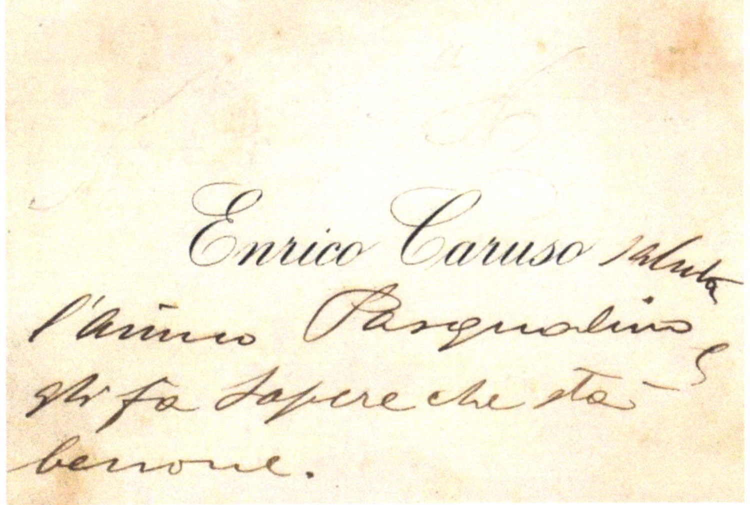

Enrico Caruso saluta
l'amico Pasqualino e
gli fa sapere che sta
benone.

"Enrico Caruso salutes the friend Pasqualino and informs him that he is very well."

Christmas 1915

A Happy New Year!
With a heart that's full of gladness,
A body full of health,
A home with naught of sadness,
And pockets full of wealth.
Caruso

Mr Pasquale I. Simonelli
c/o Italian Savings Bank
Spring St
City

GOLD MEDAL ENRICO CARUSO GAVE TO PASQUALE IMONELLI

Obverse: Caruso's profile facing left.
Lower right over shoulder: Salanto.[73]
Reverse: Muse of music[74] with lyre facing left over PER RICORDO (= memento).
On rim: TIFFANY & Co. 24 CARAT GOLD Y.

---

[73] Medal maker's signature.
[74] ? Euterpe (= *well pleasing*).

BIBLIOGRAPHY - DISCOGRAPHY

Campbell Dorcas Elisabeth, *The First Hundred Years. The Chronicle of a Mutual Savings Bank*, East River Savings Bank New York, 1949, pp. 67-69, 94.

Cannistraro, Philip V., *Mussolini, Sacco-Vanzetti, and the Anarchists: The Transatlantic Context, The Journal of Modern History*, Vol. 68, No. 1 (Mar., 1996), p. 51 n. 78.

Caruso, Enrico Jr. & FarKas, Andrew, (1990) *Enrico Caruso My Father and My Family*, Portland. Oregon: Amadeus Press Reinhard G. Pauly, General Editor.

Caruso Enrico, tenor, *Vesti la giubba*, Salvatore Cottone, piano, Recorded in Milan, 30th November 1902_Gramophone & Typewriter Company 2875

De Biasi, Agostino (Ed.), (1921) *Il Carroccio. (THE ITALIAN REVIEW). Rivista di coltura, propaganda e difesa italiana in America,* (V.7, n.1), New York: Il Carroccio Publishing Co.

De Felice Lancellotti, Vincenzina (Ed.), (1891) *VITTORIA COLONNA: PERIODICO Scientifico, Artistico, Letterario PER LE DONNE ITALIANE*, Padova: Editrice l'Unione delle DONNE COADIUTRICI della società Antoniana

familylink Search Genealogy Records, Family Trees, Military Records, Newspapers, More! http://www.lookupthe.name/italians.php?f=ln&q=Simon&p=10

Hering, C. (1904). *Ready reference tables: based on the accurate legal standard values of the United States. Volume I. Conversion factors of every unit or 1904measure in use...* (Vol. I). New York, London: J. Wiley & Sons, Chapman Hall, Limited.

Italian-American Who's-Who. A Biographical Dictionary of outstanding Italo-Americans and Italian Residents of the United States, (1935) Volume One, Published by The Vigo Press, 2 Rector Street, New York City.

Il Mattino, Italiani che onorano la Patria all'Estero. Superbo avvenire delle aziende idro-elettriche. L'attività prodigiosa del comm. Pasquale Simonelli, La Cronaca del Mezzogiorno, 15-16 Febbraio 1928.

Il Progresso italo americano, Il banchiere che portò Caruso negli USA, sezione B - supplemento illustrato della domenica, New York, 27 luglio 1986.

Italian Savings Bank, (1920?), *Italian Savings Bank. Chartered 1896,* New York City,

Jackson, Stanley, (1972) *Caruso,* First edition, New York: Stein and Day.

Key, Pierre V. R. (1922) *Enrico Caruso* a biography, Boston: Little, Brown.

Krehbiel, Henry Edward, (1909), *Chapters of opera; being historical and critical observations and records concerning the lyric drama in New York from its earliest days down to the present time,* New York, Henry Holt and co.

Robinson, Francis, (1957) *CARUSO, HIS LIFE IN PICTURES,* with Caruso Discography by John Secrist, New York and London: The Studio Publications, Inc. in association, with Thomas Y. Crowell, Company.

The Statue of Liberty-Ellis Island Foundation, Inc.
http://www.ellisisland.org/default.asp
http://www.ellisisland.org/search/FormatPassRec.asp?ID=103205050204&BN=P00320-5&sship=Oregon&lineshipid=657

Wikipedia Simonelli http://en.wikipedia.org/wiki/Main_Page
http://en.wikipedia.org/wiki/Simonelli

Wikipedia Ternina http://en.wikipedia.org/wiki/Main_Page
http://en.wikipedia.org/wiki/File:TerninaTosca.jpg

INDEX

www.ingramcontent.com/pod-product-compliance
Lightning Source LLC
LaVergne TN
LVHW052250100826
845147LV00001B/9

9780615714905